About the Authors

Dr. Wilfred Funk and Norman Lewis have both been deeply concerned with the history and use of the English language for many years. As editors, lexicographers, teachers, and authors, they have each contributed extensively to this important field. But successful as they have each been individually, their success as collaborators in producing *30 Days to a More Powerful Vocabulary* has been even greater. In various editions, at various prices, this book has sold nearly 4,000,000 copies. It is the most popular and most widely used manual of its kind produced in the twentieth century.

30 DAYS TO A MORE
POWERFUL VOCABULARY
was originally published by
Wilfred Funk, Inc.

Books by Wilfred Funk and Norman Lewis

*30 Days to a More Powerful Vocabulary

Other books by Wilfred Funk

*Six Weeks to Words of Power
The Way to Vocabulary Power and Culture
Word Origins and Their Romantic Stories

Other books by Norman Lewis

Better English
Correct Spelling Made Easy
Dictionary of Correct Spelling
Dictionary of Modern Pronunciation
How to Get More Out of Your Reading
How to Read Better and Faster
The Lewis English Refresher and Vocabulary Builder
The Modern Thesaurus of Synonyms
New Guide to Word Power
**The New Pocket Roget's Thesaurus in Dictionary Form
The New Power with Words
Power with Words
The Rapid Vocabulary Builder
RSVP—Reading, Spelling, Vocabulary, Pronunciation
*Word Power Made Easy

*Published by Pocket Books
**Published by Washington Square Press

30 Days to a More Powerful Vocabulary

WILFRED FUNK

&

NORMAN LEWIS

NEWLY REVISED BY NORMAN LEWIS

PUBLISHED BY POCKET BOOKS NEW YORK

30 DAYS TO A MORE POWERFUL VOCABULARY

Funk & Wagnalls edition published September, 1942

POCKET BOOK edition published March, 1949
61st printing..........June, 1970

Revised edition
3rd printing..........March, 1972

This revised and enlarged POCKET BOOK edition includes
every word contained in the original, higher-priced edition.
It is printed from brand-new plates made from completely reset, clear,
easy-to-read type. POCKET BOOK editions are published by
POCKET BOOKS, a division of Simon & Schuster, Inc.,
630 Fifth Avenue, New York, N.Y. 10020.
Trademarks registered in the United States and other countries.

L

To Walter M. Garcia

Contents

30 Days to
a More
Powerful
Vocabulary

Pronunciation Key

The phonetic transcription of most words in the following pages will be self-explanatory and completely clear and obvious. Only a very few symbols have to be practiced and understood before you start.

1. **ə:** *This is the phonetic symbol (called schwa) which indicates "a weak, neutral vowel sound occurring in most of the unstressed syllables in English speech, as the* a *in* alone, *the* e *in* happen, *the* u *in* circus."*

2. **ō** *The vowel sound in* gō, nō, lōw, sō, *etc.*

3. **o͞o** *The vowel sound in* fo͞ol, so͞on, no͞on, etc.

4. **zh** *The sound of the* s *in* occasion, treasure, measure, leisure, *etc.*

5. **o͝o** *The vowel sound of* bo͝ok, lo͝ok, *etc.*

Many words are stressed on more than one syllable, although only one syllable may receive the *primary* or strongest accent. When you say *pyromaniac,* for example, you place the strongest stress on the third syllable (*ma*)— that is, you say the third syllable with the greatest loudness. But the first syllable, *py,* also receives some stress; that is,

* *Funk & Wagnalls Standard College Dictionary* (New York: Funk & Wagnalls, 1968).

you say it louder than *ro, i,* or *ac*. To show these distinctions, we will capitalize and accent the strongest syllable (MAY'), and only accent the second strongest (py'). *Pyromaniac* is thus phonetically rewritten as py'-ro-MAY'-nee-ak. Further examples:

satiated: SAY'-shee-ay'-təd
archaeology: ahr'-kee-OL'-ə-jee
opinionated: ə-PIN'-yə-nay'-təd
braggadocio: brag'-ə-DŌ'-shee-ō

✕	2	3	4	5	6	7
8	9	10	11	12	13	14
15	16	17	18	19	20	21
22	23	24	25	26	27	28
29	30					

Give Us Fifteen
Minutes a Day

Your boss has a bigger vocabulary than you have.

That's one good reason why he's your boss.

This discovery has been made in the word laboratories of the world. Not by theoretical English professors, but by practical, hard-headed scientists who have been searching for the secrets of success.

After a host of experiments and years of testing they have found out:

That if your vocabulary is limited your chances of success are limited.

That one of the easiest and quickest ways to get ahead is by consciously building up your knowledge of words.

That the vocabulary of the average person almost stops growing by the middle twenties.

And that from then on it is necessary to have an intelligent plan if progress is to be made. No hit-or-miss methods will do.

It has long since been satisfactorily established that a high executive does not have a large vocabulary merely because of the opportunities of his position. That would be putting the cart before the horse. Quite the reverse is true. His skill in words was a tremendous help in getting him his job.

Dr. Johnson O'Connor of the Human Engineering Laboratory of Boston and of the Stevens Institute of Technology in Hoboken, New Jersey, gave a vocabulary test to one hundred young men who were studying to be industrial executives.

Five years later, *all,* without exception, of those who had passed in the upper 10 per cent had executive positions, while *not a single young man of the lower 25 per cent had become an executive.*

Some of the factors that lead to success can be measured as scientifically as the contents of a test tube, and it has been discovered that the one and only common characteristic of outstandingly successful people is "an extensive knowledge of the exact meaning of English words."

Vocabulary is one indication of intelligence. Learning power measurably sharpens when vocabulary increases. Here's the proof.

Two classes in a high school were selected for an experiment. The ages and background of the members of both groups were the same, and each group represented a similar cross-section of the community. One, the control class, took the normal courses. The other class had, in addition, special and rigorous vocabulary training. At the end of the period the grades of the students in the vocabulary class surpassed the grades of the members of the control group, not only in English, but in every other subject, including mathematics and the sciences.

Similarly, Professor Lewis M. Terman of Stanford University has found that a vocabulary test is as accurate a measure of intelligence as any three units of the standard and accepted Stanford-Binet I. Q. tests.

Words are the tools of thinking. It naturally follows,

then, that the more words you have at your command, the clearer and more accurate your thinking will be.

Words are your medium of exchange, the coin with which you do business with all those around you. With words you relate to people, communicate your feelings and thoughts to them, influence them, persuade them, control them. In short, through words you shape your own destiny. For your words are your personality; your vocabulary is you.

Words are explosive. Phrases are packed with TNT. A single word can destroy a friendship, can start or end a marital battle, can land a large order. The right phrases in the mouths of clerks have quadrupled the sales of a department store. The wrong words used by a campaign orator have lost an election. Four unfortunate words—"Rum, Romanism, and Rebellion"—used in a Republican campaign speech threw the Catholic vote and the Presidential victory to Grover Cleveland.

Armies fight for phrases: "Make the world safe for Democracy"; "V for Victory"; "Remember Pearl Harbor."

Words have changed the direction of history. Words can also change the direction of your life. They can raise a man from mediocrity to success.

We submit that if you methodically increase your vocabulary you will improve your chances for success.

This book enlists active cooperation, continuous written and oral response. It will test you every step of the way, it will demand unceasing feedback from you, and thus it will make words your friends and allies.

We expect to prove to you that developing a rich and robust vocabulary can be both fun and challenging.

Give us fifteen minutes a day, and we will guarantee that at the end of a month, when you have turned over the last page of this book, your words, your reading, your conversation, and your life will all have a new and deeper meaning for you.

For words can make you great!

╳	╳	3	4	5	6	7
8	9	10	11	12	13	14
15	16	17	18	19	20	21
22	23	24	25	26	27	28
29	30					

Take This Twelve-Minute Test of Your Verbal Power

First, we will take your word portrait.

When the picture is finished, you will know how you look to others as a conversationalist and how you may appear when you write a simple social note or a business letter.

The lines of your likeness that are to be drawn here will indicate the extent of your vocabulary, the facility with which you can recall and use words, and the knowledge that you have of their precise meanings. There will also be brief spelling and pronunciation tests so that we can get a complete picture.

You will find the tests in this chapter simple and entertaining. They will take exactly twelve minutes, and when you are through and have checked your score, you will know what's wrong, if anything, with your vocabulary and your use of words. You will, in short, have painted your own word portrait. Then, in the chapters that follow, we

6

will show you how to strengthen any weak points that may have appeared.

How do words treat you? Are you comfortable with them? Do they come easily to you? When you write and speak, do your words paint the sort of picture of you that will do you the most good in this highly competitive world? Does your language usually present a true reflection of your mind, your emotions, and your personality? Or does it sometimes betray you and blur your thoughts? Do people occasionally misunderstand you? Or can you compel them to listen, react, obey?

Like everyone else, you want certain things from life. No matter what those benefits are, or what particular way you have chosen to go about getting them, you know that your first and most effective means will be the words you use.

In short, the satisfaction and the success you get out of life depend very greatly on the skill with which you communicate your needs, your desires, your opinions to others.

Ready to discover what your command of language says about you?

TEST I
Verbal Speed (Elementary)

DIRECTIONS: Write in the blank space next to each of the words in the following list another word *that begins with S* and has a meaning directly *opposite* to the given word.
Time: 60 seconds

EXAMPLE: fast   slow
    sweet   sour
    buy   sell

START TIMING: 1. tall   S................
      2. north   S................
      3. happy   S................
      4. different   S................
      5. dangerous   S................

   6. big   S........
   7. dull   S........
   8. noisy   S........
   9. sit   S........
  10. receive   S........
              End Timing
(Answers for all tests will be found at the end of the
  chapter.)

You have just been tested for fluency.

You should have breezed through this test at high speed
in less than sixty seconds with no hesitancy and no mistakes. If you had to think for more than an instant to recall
the proper word, it is likely that you experience some difficulty in expressing your thoughts. You are probably
seeing men who are not as bright as you getting ahead of
you. You may often wonder: "What have they got that I
haven't got?"

Your lack of an adequate word arsenal may have seriously handicapped you. If so, this book is designed for
you. It will give you the chance to go to work and overcome your obstacle.

TEST II
Verbal Speed (Advanced)

DIRECTIONS: As in the previous test, write a word beginning with S which is *opposite* in meaning to each of the
  following.

              Time: 90 seconds

START TIMING: 1. generous   S........
               2. meaningless   S........
               3. believing   S........
               4. complicated   S........
               5. doubtful   S........
               6. careful   S........
               7. wakefulness   S........

8. rough   S........
9. objective   S................
10. laugh   S..........
End Timing

Speed and accuracy are again of great importance. If you completed this test in ninety seconds and got eight out of ten correct, you are far above the average and you doubtless show unusual skill and ease in translating your thoughts into the proper words; you are going to make swift progress in the lessons that are ahead.

If, on the other hand, you exceeded your time limit, or if you were wrong in five or more words, it is critically necessary that you start today to improve your vocabulary. We are dealing in this book with one of the richest languages in the world, and with a little practice and patience you can easily make its great wealth your own.

TEST III
Synonym Recall

Here is a test of your skill from another point of view. You have been working with *antonyms,* or words of opposite meanings. How will you do with *synonyms,* or words of the same, or almost the same, meanings? It is highly important that you have a wealth of synonyms, which are analogous to the many colors on an artist's palette, at your command. Synonyms within easy reach help you paint for your listener the many shades of your thoughts; they lend variety and interest to your conversation and writing.

DIRECTIONS: In the spaces given below write two words that are synonymous with the given word.
Time: 2 minutes

EXAMPLE: beautiful   lovely, pretty
         strong   rugged, powerful
         short   brief, concise
This test should be finished within the time limit, as

there are many more than two synonyms for each of these words. Check with a dictionary if your answers are not found in the list at the end of the chapter.

START TIMING:
1. defects (*noun*) ....
2. desires (*noun*) ....
3. true ....
4. suitable ....
5. luminous ....
6. loathing (*noun*) ....
7. doubtful ....
8. vulgar ....
9. admiration ....
10. very ....

End Timing

TEST IV
Synonym Recognition

We have tested your ability to recall the synonyms for a given word. We are now going to test your ability to *recognize* synonyms when you see them.

DIRECTIONS: In the following list there are sixteen words. Start with *infidel* and put a small figure 1 above it. Run through the list until you find another word that has the same or similar meaning. Put a 1 above that one. Then try the second word on the list, *large,* putting a figure 2 above it, and search for a word of similar meaning and mark it 2. And so on until you have eight pairs of synonyms or words of similar meaning.

Time: 90 seconds

START TIMING:
infidel	ingenious	occur	aberration
large	happen	persuade	kidnap
bulky	eccentricity	clever	unbeliever
abduct	unsophisticated	induce	ingenuous

End Timing

TEST V
Homonyms

DIRECTIONS: Homonyms are words that are pronounced almost exactly alike but that differ considerably in meaning. Check the homonym that makes sense in each of the following sentences.

Time: 90 seconds

START TIMING:

1. Why does modern music have such a strange [(a) *affect*, (b) *effect*] on you?
2. Most buildings have [(a) *stationery*, (b) *stationary*] walls.
3. The [(a) *principal*, (b) *principle*] features of Southern California are sunshine and smog.
4. Sitting contentedly by the fire, the cat licked [(a) *it's*, (b) *its*] paws.
5. His vocal [(a) *cords*, (b) *chords*] are inflamed.
6. He sat for hours [(a) *poring*, (b) *pouring*] over the dictionary.
7. He listened with [(a) *baited*, (b) *bated*] breath for the second shoe to fall.
8. Admiral Nelson is famous for one of the most important [(a) *navel*, (b) *naval*] encounters in British history.
9. The scene of the accident was lighted by a huge [(a) *flare*, (b) *flair*].
10. The boxer made a [(a) *feint*, (b) *faint*] with his left.

End Timing

TEST VI
Understanding Words

DIRECTIONS: Check the definition that properly explains the italicized word in each phrase.

Time: 2 minutes

START TIMING:

1. An *acrimonious* argument
   (a) long-winded
   (b) sharp, biting, sarcastic
   (c) dull, pointless, and incoherent
2. A *soporific* lecture
   (a) so boring as to put one to sleep
   (b) brilliant and informative
   (c) well-attended
3. *Panacea* for social ills
   (a) direct cause
   (b) cure-all
   (c) condition encouraging continuation
4. An *evanescent* feeling
   (a) fading away quickly
   (b) composed of both dread and desire
   (c) so unique that it is experienced by very few people
5. Overwhelmed by *ennui*
   (a) fear
   (b) dissatisfaction and boredom resulting from inactivity
   (c) a sudden awareness of one's unconscious motivation
6. A *facetious* remark
   (a) witty or joking at an inappropriate time
   (b) tending to make peace between people in conflict
   (c) totally irrelevant to the situation
7. A *maelstrom* of emotions
   (a) complete lack
   (b) catalogue in chronological order
   (c) violent, stormy confusion
8. *Maudlin* attitudes
   (a) self-destructive
   (b) tearfully and excessively sentimental
   (c) showing great maturity at a surprisingly early age

9. Drove *adroitly*
   - (a) skillfully
   - (b) nervously
   - (c) inattentively
10. A *sardonic* smile
    - (a) empty, meaningless
    - (b) open and trusting
    - (c) bitter and scornful

End Timing

TEST VII
Spelling Without Error

Here are ten common words frequently misspelled by those whose linguistic ability needs sharpening. Check the form that looks right to you.

Time: 60 seconds

START TIMING:

1. (a) occurrance, (b) occurrence, (c) occurance
2. (a) ecstasy, (b) ecstacy, (c) extacy
3. (a) drunkeness, (b) drunkenness, (c) drunkedness
4. (a) embarassing, (b) embarrassing, (c) embarrasing
5. (a) irresistible, (b) irresistable, (c) irrisistible
6. (a) supersede, (b) supercede, (c) superceed
7. (a) disappoint, (b) dissapoint, (c) dissappoint
8. (a) occassional, (b) occasional, (c) ocassional
9. (a) indispensable, (b) indispensible, (c) indespensible
10. (a) perseverance, (b) perseverence, (c) perserverance

End Timing

TEST VIII
Pronouncing in the Educated Manner

The pronunciation of American English is, admittedly, unstable: the sound of words changes according to geographical area, ethnic background, economic and social levels, etc. *Mary, marry,* and *merry,* for example, are pronounced almost identically in the Midwest and along much of the Pacific coastal regions; whereas in the East and South they sound very different. The first syllable of *orange* is pronounced *or* in California and *are* in New York. The vowel sound of *talk* and *walk* is uttered one way by a native of Brooklyn and quite another way by someone born in Los Angeles. Words like *either, tomato, tune, adult, licorice, strength,* and many others can often show the age, income, background, and sophistication of the speaker.

Nevertheless, one kind of pronunciation test will be useful in completing your verbal portrait. The following ten words, among many others, have both an illiterate or dialectal and an educated pronunciation. Say each one carefully according to its phonetic respelling, then check the form that sounds most nearly like what you ordinarily use in conversation.

The symbol ə is the sound of the *a* in *about* or in *Linda.*

Time: 90 seconds

START TIMING:

1. genuine   (a) JEN'-yə-win
             (b) JEN'-yə-wyne

2. athlete   (a) ATH'-ə-leet
             (b) ATH'-leet

3. film   (a) FILM
             (b) FIL'-əm

4. modern   (a) MAHR'-dən
             (b) MOD'-rən
             (c) MOD'-ərn

5. accept   (a) ək-SEPT′
            (b) ə-SEPT′
6. drowned   (a) DROWN′-dəd
            (b) DROWND
7. wrestle   (a) RESS′-əl
            (b) RASS′-əl
8. pattern   (a) PAT′-rən
            (b) PAT′-ərn
9. figure   (a) FIG′-yər
            (b) FIG′-ər
10. attacked   (a) ə-TAK′-təd
            (b) ə-TAKT′

End Timing

Now you may relax. Your test of verbal power is concluded; your word portrait is finished. What you will see on the canvas—pleasant or unpleasant, encouraging or discouraging—is what the world sees when you write or speak. At this point, before you check your score, we offer you one important thought: No matter how good or bad your word power is today, it can be immeasurably better, more useful, more potent, in just thirty days.

Scoring and Interpretation

Determine your score for each test by comparing your answers with those given below:

TEST I:

(1) short; (2) south; (3) sad; (4) same, similar; (5) safe; (6) small; (7) smart, sharp, sparkling; (8) silent, still; (9) stand; (10) send

Scoring: 2 points for each correct answer
           Maximum score: 20 points
                Your Score: ....

TEST II:

(1) selfish, stingy; (2) sensible, significant; (3) skeptical, suspicious; (4) simple; (5)

sure; (6) slipshod, slovenly, sloppy; (7)
sleep, sleepiness, slumber, somnolence; (8)
smooth; (9) subjective; (10) sob, scowl
Scoring: 2 points for each correct answer
                Maximum score: 20 points
                                    Your Score: ....

TEST III:

(1) shortcomings, imperfections, faults,
    weaknesses, deficiencies, blemishes

(2) wishes, wants, longings, cravings, ap-
    petites

(3) right, correct, truthful, genuine,
    straight, honest, faithful, veracious,
    pure

(4) appropriate, consistent, fitting, fit, ap-
    plicable

(5) bright, lustrous, radiant, brilliant, vivid,
    gleaming, shining, glowing, lucid

(6) disgust, aversion, detestation, antipa-
    thy, repugnance, abhorrence

(7) ambiguous, vague, obscure, indefinite,
    loose, uncertain, dubious, question-
    able, dubitable

(8) rude, common, coarse, gross, ill-bred,
    low, obscene, ill-mannered, crass

(9) praise, approval, commendation, es-
    teem, veneration, approbation

(10) extremely, exceedingly, highly, enor-
    mously, immensely, abundantly, ter-
    ribly, quite

Scoring: 2 points for each question answered
            correctly
            Failure to give 2 synonyms counts
            zero
            Maximum score: 20 points
                                    Your Score: ....

TEST IV:

| (1) infidel | (1) unbeliever |
| (2) ingenious | (2) clever |

(3) occur	(3) happen
(4) aberration	(4) eccentricity
(5) large	(5) bulky
(6) persuade	(6) induce
(7) kidnap	(7) abduct
(8) unsophisticated	(8) ingenuous

Scoring: 2 points for each correct pair
Maximum score: 16 points
Your Score: ....

TEST V:
(1) b; (2) b; (3) a; (4) b; (5) a; (6) a;
(7) b; (8) b; (9) a; (10) a
Scoring: 1 point for each correct choice
Maximum score: 10 points
Your Score: ....

TEST VI:
(1) b; (2) a; (3) b; (4) a; (5) b; (6) a;
(7) c; (8) b; (9) a; (10) c
Scoring: 2 points for each correct choice
Maximum score: 20 points
Your Score: ....

TEST VII:
(1) b; (2) a; (3) b; (4) b; (5) a; (6) a;
(7) a; (8) b; (9) a; (10) a
Scoring: 2 points for each correct choice
Maximum score: 20 points
Your Score: ....

TEST VIII:
(1) a; (2) b; (3) a; (4) c; (5) a; (6) b;
(7) a; (8) b; (9) a; (10) b
Scoring: 2 points for each correct choice
Maximum score: 20 points
Your Score: ....

Now add your scores
in the 8 tests to
arrive at   *Your Total Score:* ....
out of a maximum of
146.

Interpretation

YOUR TOTAL SCORE:

120–146   You belong in the top 10 per cent of the literate population of this country and you should be on the way to a high position in your vocational, intellectual, and social life. You will get a special pleasure out of this book as you perfect a vocabulary that is already sound.

99–119   Your vocabulary is about average and is therefore not helping you gain success as fast as you might otherwise be able to. Why not begin today to overcome an unnecessary handicap? Start building your vocabulary now and make this interesting work a daily habit. The new words you learn will acquaint you with new fields of knowledge, and there will be many additional subtle and indirect rewards. Remember: There is no easier way to achieve success than by adding to your vocabulary.

98 and   This score shows a definitely impoverished
below   vocabulary; your weakness in words may be holding you back. It would be a foolish and fatal mistake not to do something immediately about it. Here are two don'ts for you: Don't let your low score unduly disturb you. And don't feel that only a university graduate can be an expert user of words. Shakespeare attended school for ten years all told. Robert Burns, the Scottish poet, was a day laborer without education. Neither Charles Lamb nor Charles Dickens had enough formal schooling to talk about. And Abraham Lincoln didn't know what the inside of a school looked like. They and many others like them became mas-

ters of speech. They achieved their effectiveness by industry and practice. So can you. And when you do, your reward will be great.

The beauty of this book is that you start to benefit—not after months of trial—but from the first day and with the first chapter.

X	X	X	4	5	6	7
8	9	10	11	12	13	14
15	16	17	18	19	20	21
22	23	24	25	26	27	28
29	30					

The Romance
of Words

From now on we want you to look at words intently, to be inordinately curious about them and to examine them syllable by syllable, letter by letter. They are your tools of understanding and self-expression. Collect them. Keep them in condition. Learn how to handle them. Develop a fastidious, but not a fussy, choice. Work always toward good taste in their use. Train your ear for their harmonies.

We urge you not to take words for granted just because they have been part of your daily speech since childhood. You must examine them. Turn them over and over as though you were handling a coin, and see the seal and superscription on each one. *We would like you actually to fall in love with words.*

Words are not dead things. They are fairly wriggling with life. They are the exciting and mysterious tokens of our thoughts, and like human beings, they are born, come to maturity, grow old, and die, and sometimes they are even reborn in a new age. A word, from its birth to its death, is a process, not a static thing.

Words, like living trees, have roots, branches, and leaves.

Shall we stay with this analogy for a few moments, and see how perfect it is?

The story of the root of a word is the story of its origin. The study of origins is called *etymology*, which in turn has *its* roots in the Greek word *etymon*, meaning "true or original meaning," and the Greek ending *-logia*, meaning "science or study." So *etymology* means the science or study of true or original meanings.

Every word in our language is a frozen metaphor, a frozen picture. It is this poetry behind words that gives language its overwhelming power. And the more intimately we know the romance that lies within each word, the better understanding we will have of its meaning.

For instance, on certain occasions you will probably say that you have "calculated" the cost of something or other. What does the term *calculate* really mean? Here is the story. Years ago, ancient Romans had an instrument called a *hodometer*, or "road measurer," which corresponded to our modern taxi meter. If you had hired a two-wheeled Roman vehicle to ride, say, to the Forum, you might have found in the back a tin can with a revolving cover that held a quantity of pebbles. This can was so contrived that each time the wheel turned, the metal cover also revolved, and a pebble dropped through a hole into the receptacle below. At the end of your trip you counted the pebbles and *calculated* your bill. You see, the Latin word for pebble was *calculus*, and that's where our word "calculate" comes from.

There are, of course, many words with much simpler histories than this. When you speak of a *surplus*, for instance, you are merely saying that you have a *sur* (French for "over") *plus* (French for "more") or a *sur-plus*. That is, you have an "over-more" than you need.

Should you be in a snooty mood for the nonce, and happen to look at someone rather haughtily, your friends might call you *supercilious*, a word that comes from the Latin *supercilium*, meaning that "eyebrow" you just raised.

cum — with

That person you are so fond of, who has become your *companion*, is simply one who eats bread with you—from Latin *cum*, "with," and *panis*, "bread." *Trumps* in bridge is from the French *triomphe* or "triumph," an old-time game of cards. In modern cards, one suit is allowed to triumph over, or to "trump" the other suits. And still again, in the army, the *lieutenant* is literally one who takes the place of the captain when the latter is not around—from the French *lieu* (we use it in "in lieu of") and *tenir*, "to hold." The *captain*, in turn, derives from the Latin word *caput* ("head"). *Colonel* comes from *columna* (the "column" that he leads).

If, by any chance, you would like to twit your friend, the Wall Street *broker*, just tell him that his professional title came from the Middle English word *brocour*, a "broacher," or one who opens, or broaches, a cask to draw off the wine or liquor. We still employ the same word in the original sense when we say "He broached [or opened up] the subject." The broacher, or broker, became in time a salesman of wine, then of other things, such as stocks and bonds.

These are the roots of words. We next come to the branches. The branches of our language tree are those many groups of words that have grown out from one original root.

Let's take an example. From the Latin root *spectare*, which means "to look," more than 240 English words have sprouted. We find the root in such words as *spectacle* (those things you look through), *spectator* (one who looks or watches), *respect* (the tribute you give to a person you care to look at again), and *inspect* (to look into). When you treat someone with *disrespect*, you make it plain that you do not care to look at him again (*dis*, "not"—*re*, "again"—*spect*, "look"). *Introspection* is a looking within.

Turning to the Greek language, which has so largely enriched our own, we discover *graphein*, "to write," another prolific source of English words. We have *telegraph* (writing from a distance), *phonograph* (writing by sound), *photograph* (writing by means of light), *stenographer* (one who does condensed writing), and *mimeograph* (to write a copy or imitation).

We have in our language a host of roots such as these. There is the Latin *spirare,* meaning "to blow or breathe," from which we get such English words as *inspire* (breathe into), *expire* (breathe out), *perspire* (breathe through), *respiration* (breathing again or often).

Our word "liable" comes from the Latin *ligare,* "to bind." This fascinating root has branched out into *oblige* and *obligate* (to bind to do something), *ligature* (bandage or binding), *ligament* (something that ties two things together), and, with the root no longer so obvious, *league* (those nations or other organizations that are bound together), and even the word *ally* (to bind to one another), which is from *ad* and *ligare.*

These, then, are the branches. We turn now to the leaves. If the roots are the origins of words and the branches are the word families that stem out of them, the leaves of this language tree would be the words themselves and their meanings.

Each given word, in its beginning, had, no doubt, only one meaning. But words are so full of life that they are continually sprouting the green shoots of new meanings.

Shall we choose just one word as an instance of the amazing vitality of language? The simple three-letter word *run,* up to this moment of writing, has more than ninety dictionary definitions. There are the *run* in your stocking, the *run* on the bank, and a *run* in baseball. The clock may *run* down, but you *run* up a bill. Colors *run.* You may *run* a race or *run* a business. You may have the *run* of the mill, or, quite different, the *run* of the house when you get the *run* of things. And this dynamic little word, we can assure you, has just begun its varied career with these examples.

Is it any wonder that our unabridged dictionaries contain hundreds of thousands of living and usable words, words sparkling with life, prolific in their breeding, luxuriant in their growth, continually shifting and changing in their meanings?

Words even have definite personalities and characters.

They can be sweet, sour, discordant, musical. They can be sugary or acrid, soft or sharp, hostile or friendly.

From this time on, as we enter our word studies, try to become keenly aware of words. Look at them, if possible, with the fresh eyes of one who is seeing them for the first time. If we have persuaded you to do this, you will then be on the way to the success that can be won with a more powerful vocabulary.

✗	✗	✗	✗	5	6	7
8	9	10	11	12	13	14
15	16	17	18	19	20	21
22	23	24	25	26	27	28
29	30					

Words for Mature Minds

I

There are words in English that can be understood only by those who have lived and become mature. No explanation, no definitions could make them clear to a child.

Here are ten such words. Pronounce each one aloud several times, following carefully the phonetic respelling. (Recall that the symbol ə has the sound of the *a* in *about* or in *Linda*.)

1. *vicarious* (vy-KAIR'-ee-əs)
2. *rationalize* (RASH'-ən-ə-lize)
3. *gregarious* (grə-GAIR'-ee-əs)
4. *obsequious* (əb-SEE'-kwee-əs)
5. *maudlin* (MAWD'-lin)
6. *ascetic* (a-SET'-ik)
7. *pander* (PAN'-dər)
8. *sublimate* (SUB'-lə-mate)
9. *wanton* (WAHN'-tən)
10. *effete* (ə-FEET')

II

You might find it hard, perhaps absolutely impossible, to explain these terms to a nine-year-old boy or girl.

But you, an adult, will be able to comprehend them and to make them your property.

Let us discuss them, one by one. Here and there we will give you the etymology of the word, if its history is interesting and happens to throw any light on its present-day meaning.

1. *Vicarious.* This is an abstract word, but it is one that is easy for the grown-up mind to grasp. For example, there are two ways to travel: one by buying a steamship ticket and going to your destination, say Paris; the other by reading travel stories or travel circulars *about* Paris. In the first instance you have enjoyed your travel experience *directly.* In the second instance you have enjoyed it *vicariously.*

A child is learning about life when he "pretends," when he plays "store," or "house," or "doctor." Of course he is fully living the life that children do, but he is also living adult life, not directly, but *vicariously.* And owing to his emotional immaturity, he is not ready, at his age, to grasp the difference, in thought and effect, between actual living and *vicarious* living. When he is older and more mature he will live less *vicariously* and more actually, and then he will be able to appreciate the significance of the word.

You, as an older person, will recognize that you are escaping from the real world and are living for the moment a *vicarious* existence and are having *vicarious* joys and sorrows when you are reading a book. You are living, not your own life, but the lives of the characters of the story. The lonely, friendless woman living a life of suffocating routine or hopeless boredom can sit glued, hour after hour, to the television set. She then becomes the lovely young girl to whom a virile male makes passionate love; she can experience *vicariously* all the excitement, romance, thrills, exotic adventure that her real life is so empty of. She can be a spy, a murderer, a figure of international intrigue, a visitor from another planet. She has only to twist the dial and change her drab existence into an abundant, fulfilling, and electric (but *vicarious*) reality.

2. *Rationalize.* You, as a human being, tend to *rationalize*. So do all of us. There are selfish men, for instance, who will never give anything to charity. They don't wish to regard themselves as selfish, however. They prefer to think that charity is harmful to the poor and demoralizes those who receive it. In this way the miser can save his money and his face at the same time. He is *rationalizing* his selfish act and the *rationalization* makes him feel better.

In similar fashion, a father who is angry may spank his boy merely to relieve his own personal feelings. But in self-defense he will *rationalize* his action by making himself believe that the spanking has been done for the good of the child.

The term *rationalize* has a number of meanings, but the most common one refers to the unconscious process of thought by which one justifies a discreditable act, and by which one offers to oneself and the world a better motive for one's action than the true motive.

3. *Gregarious.* This term comes from the Latin word *grex*, "a flock," as of sheep, and you know sheep like to stay together. If you are a *gregarious* type, you are a friendly person, a good mixer; you like to be with other people. That is, you are the extremely sociable kind. Because you are *gregarious* you enjoy parties, crowded theaters and dance floors; you like to be where folks flock in small or large numbers. Because people are *gregarious,* they get married, have families, live in thronging cities, sing and play together. A hunger for love or friendship and a feeling of kinship with other human beings are normal and common human traits. It is the herd instinct that makes people, to a greater or lesser degree, *gregarious*.

4. *Obsequious.* The beggar, the underling, the lackey, and the flunkey all tend to be *obsequious*. Those who wait

on others in an inferior capacity and whose lives and jobs depend on the whims of their masters are apt to be cringing and fawning. They are often excessively, sickeningly, and insincerely polite. If your waiter in a restaurant believes that you are the type who will tip him well, watch how *obsequious* he will be, how he will bow to you and attend on your slightest wish. If you don't leave the expected tip, however, his *obsequiousness* will quickly vanish and he will not (*ob,* "upon," *sequor,* "follow") follow submissively upon your wishes.

5. *Maudlin.* A *maudlin* person is one who is super-sentimental and gushing, who cries easily and without much cause. People who are *maudlin* in their affections usually overdo the act, and their love becomes tiresome and offensive. The word *maudlin* can also be applied to those who have been made foolish and silly by too much drinking.

Here, incidentally, is an odd word history. Mary Magdalene, who washed the feet of Christ, has often been pictured with her eyes red from weeping. In time, the name Magdalene was contracted into the adjective *maudlin.*

6. *Ascetic.* The *ascetic* is one who is given to severe self-denial and austerity, one who practices rigid abstinence, often for religious reasons. When you say that a man is an *ascetic,* you mean that he is one who shuns all the luxuries and physical pleasures of life. Anyone who eats and drinks heartily or who otherwise dissipates is the precise opposite of an *ascetic,* and does not believe in *asceticism* (a-SET′-ə-siz-əm).

7. *Pander.* This verb literally means to minister to the gratification of the passions and prejudices of others, usually to one's own profit. Novels that give blow-by-blow descriptions of bedroom intimacies, and motion pictures and TV shows that omit none of the gory details of violence, torture, and murder have been accused of *pandering* to the so-called base instincts and morbid curiosity of their readers and audience. Ruthless dictators of the past are said to have *pandered* to the lowest instincts of the mobs, to self-

ishness, cruelty, and greed, in order to gain power. *Pander,* therefore, is an unpleasant word with an unpleasant meaning. The noun *panderer* has a still more restricted meaning and frequently signifies a man who procures women for others, just as Pandarus, the leader of the Lycians in the Trojan war, is said to have procured the lovely lady Cressida for Troilus.

8. *Sublimate.* This word originally came from the Latin *sublimatus,* "raised on high," and is closely related to "sublime." When the energies of a potential hoodlum or gangster are channeled into athletic games, into a business career, or into some other useful endeavor, his former destructive activities are said to have been *sublimated.* Psychologists tell us that unfulfilled sexual needs are often *sublimated* into creative activities in art or poetry, that the surgeon or butcher may be a *sublimated* sadist, that the psychopathic exhibitionist becomes an actor. To *sublimate,* then, is to express primitive and socially unacceptable drives in constructive ways, usually through completely unconscious processes. A female whose unconscious desire it is to enslave men, to dominate and destroy all males, becomes the energetic and successful business executive or the president of a college with a largely male faculty, and only her psychiatrist knows that she is *sublimating.*

9. *Wanton.* Call a woman *wanton* and you are saying that she indulges every passion, that she is lewd and lascivious—in short that she believes in living it up, with no thought of consequences or of the morrow's hangover. She never expects to be sorry in the morning, and she never is.

10. *Effete.* When animals, plants, or soil are worn out and incapable of producing, they are called *effete* (Latin *ex,* "out," *fetus,* "having produced"). More commonly, though, this adjective is applied to humans or their institutions, and when you refer to ancient Rome at the time of its fall as an *effete* civilization, you mean that it was degenerate, worn out, sterile, devoid of vigor, weakened by luxury, self-indulgence, and soft living.

III

Now we want to help you make these ten words your own possession, your private property. Below, in the column on the right, are the definitions of the ten terms we are studying in this chapter. Take your pencil and write each word next to its definition.

1. M .... tearfully or excessively sentimental
2. P .... to cater to base desires
3. G .... preferring the company of others to solitude
4. E .... spent; exhausted; barren of energy; worn out by rich or effortless existence
5. A .... practicing extreme self-denial
6. V .... enjoyed by one person through his sympathetic but indirect participation in the experience of another (real or fictional) person; substitutional
7. R .... to attribute one's actions to rational and creditable motives, without an adequate analysis of the true and usually unconscious motives
8. O .... servilely attentive; fawning
9. S .... to direct energy from its primitive and destructive aim to one that is culturally or ethically higher and therefore socially acceptable
10. W .... unchaste; lewd; licentious; marked by arrogant recklessness of justice, of the feelings of others, or the like; also, having no just provocation; wilfully malicious

ANSWERS: (1) maudlin; (2) pander; (3) gregarious; (4) effete; (5) ascetic; (6) vicarious; (7)

rationalize; (8) obsequious; (9) sublimate;
(10) wanton

IV

Keep your pencil always ready. This is a workbook, a
self-teaching manual, and we want you to write in it continually. The only way you can feel at home with new
words is by saying them, writing them, using them.

Now take the following eight words and change them
into other parts of speech according to the instructions. Be
sure in each case that the resulting sentence or phrase
makes sense.

1. Change *vicarious* to an adverb, as, *He trav-
eled* ....

2. Change *rationalize* to a noun, as, *You are guilty
of* ....

3. Change *gregarious* to a noun, as *No one doubts
the* .... *of human beings.*

4. Change *obsequious* to an adverb, as, *He obeyed*
....

5. Change *ascetic* to a noun referring to the philosophy
or practice, as, *He is a believer in* ....

6. Change *pander* to a noun, as, *He is a* .... *to
the greed of others.*

7. Change *sublimate* to an adjective, as, *His* ....
passion gives power to his poetry.

8. Change *wanton* to a noun, as, *Hers was a life
characterized by* ....

ANSWERS: (1) vicariously; (2) rationalization; (3)
gregariousness; (4) obsequiously; (5) asceticism; (6) panderer; (7) sublimated;
(8) wantonness

V

From your work so far with these ten words, you should
now have a fairly good idea of how they may be used in

sentences, even if you may have met some of them for the
first time. Test yourself. Without referring to the list on the
previous page, try to fill in the required word in the sentences that follow. Note that any one of the several
forms of each word may be needed. Use your pencil: the
mere physical act of writing a word will help to fix it in
your mind.

1. Marie is too .... to be happy without friends.
2. The waiter bowed .... to every wealthy cus-
   tomer who came in the restaurant.
3. His dissipated life has sapped his ambition and
   health and made him ....
4. The motion picture was so sickeningly ....
   that most of the audience left in disgust.
5. Mothers feel a .... pleasure in their children's
   accomplishments.
6. Be honest with yourself. Don't try to ....
   what you are doing.
7. He lived the life of an ...., for he abhorred
   self-indulgence and luxury.
8. The dishonest politician .... to the greed and
   thoughtlessness of the mob.
9. Some say that all great art is a .... of primitive instincts.
10. She led a fruitless, ..., uncontrolled life.

ANSWERS: (1) gregarious; (2) obsequiously; (3) ef-
         fete; (4) maudlin; (5) vicarious; (6) ra-
         tionalize; (7) ascetic; (8) panders; (9)
         sublimation; (10) wanton

VI
True or False?

Are you feeling more and more power and understanding? Try two more exercises to reinforce your learning.
Check your reaction to each statement.

1. Psychoanalysts encourage their patients to *rationalize*.   True...... False......
2. *Gregarious* people avoid social gatherings.   True...... False......
3. A haughty person is necessarily *obsequious*.   True...... False......
4. *Vicarious* experiences are naturally more satisfying than real ones.   True...... False......
5. Intoxicated people often become *maudlin*.   True...... False......
6. *Asceticism* is a popular practice among wealthy Americans.   True...... False......
7. Men of strong ethics and integrity usually *pander* to the desires of others.   True...... False......
8. *Sublimation* is a self-destructive practice.   True...... False......
9. During its latter period, Ancient Rome was noted for *wanton* excesses.   True...... False......
10. One becomes *effete* through self-discipline and careful restraint.   True...... False......

ANSWERS: All false except 5 and 9.

VII
Same or Opposite?

Is each pair of words essentially the same or more nearly opposite in meaning? Check your quick reaction.

1. vicarious—actual   Same ...... Opposite ......
2. rationalization—justification   Same ...... Opposite ......
3. gregarious—solitary   Same ...... Opposite ......
4. obsequious—rude   Same ...... Opposite ......
5. maudlin—unsentimental   Same ...... Opposite ......

6. asceticism—luxury   Same ...... Opposite ....✓..
7. pander—cater   Same ..✓.. Opposite ......
8. wanton—restrained   Same ...... Opposite ...✓..
9. effete—vigorous   Same ...... Opposite ....✓.
10. sublimated—detoured   Same ..✓... Opposite ......

ANSWERS: (1) opposite;   (2) same;   (3) opposite;
          (4) opposite;   (5) opposite;   (6) opposite;
          (7) same;   (8) opposite;   (9) opposite;
          (10) same

VIII

Remember this: Once an adult has finished his schooling, he rarely adds more than twenty-five new words to his
vocabulary each year thereafter. Already, in one session,
you have at least increased your knowledge of these ten
words, even though you may have met them before.
Therefore, whenever you add ten new words to your
vocabulary you have done almost as much as most people
do in six months.

Be sure, though, that you *keep* these words. Can you
recall all ten of them now without referring to the text?
Here they are in random order, with only the initial letters
to prod your memory. When you have them all down,
check your spelling against the list on pages 24–25 and
pronounce them aloud.

1. E ....   6. W ....
2. A ....   7. O ....
3. M ....   8. R ....
4. V ....   9. S ....
5. P ....   10. G ....

Words About Doctors and Specialists

Of course you know that you have two different kinds of vocabulary, and that one is much larger than the other.

Your *recognition* vocabulary is made up of the words that you can "recognize" and understand when you read them or hear them spoken.

Your *functional* vocabulary includes the words that you recall and use when *you yourself* speak.

Your recognition vocabulary is about three times as large as your functional vocabulary.

If, as an example, you study French and you learn merely to read that language, you will find that you will be unable to speak it because you are practiced only in recognizing the words in print, but not in recalling them when you don't see them.

Or, conversely, if you are taught only to speak French, you will fail when it comes to reading the language because you have not had any practice in understanding or "recognizing" the printed words.

In order to develop both types of vocabulary it is there-

fore important that you not only *read* the words that are
new to you in this book and *write* them down, but that
you say them aloud many times, pronouncing them according to the phonetic respelling following each word.

I

In this chapter we discuss the terms for various specialists in the healing professions.

1. The *obstetrician* (ob'-stə-TRISH'-ən) provides care
for pregnant women, delivers babies, and gives post-natal
attention to mothers. He practices *obstetrics* (ob-STET'-
riks). (Almost all *obstetricians* are also *gynecologists*—see
word 8, below.)

2. The *pediatrician* (pee'-dee-ə-TRISH'-ən) takes over
after the obstetrician. He specializes in the treatment of
infants and very young children; he practices *pediatrics*
(pee'-dee-AT'-riks).

3. The *podiatrist* (pə-DY'-ə-trist) treats the minor ailments of your feet. More popularly, he is called a chiropodist (kə-ROP'-ə-dist). The practice or profession is
podiatry (pə-DY'-ə-tree) or *chiropody* (kə-ROP'-ə-dee).

4. The *osteopath* (OSS'-tee-ə-path') works on the theory that diseases arise chiefly from the displacement of
bones, with resultant pressure on nerve centers and blood
vessels. Hence, his treatment is manipulation of the affected parts. (However, some *osteopaths* also practice
general medicine, obstetrics, pediatrics, etc.) He practices
osteopathy (oss'-tee-OP'-ə-thee).

5. The *ophthalmologist* (off'-thal-MOL'-ə-jist) is a
medical doctor and often a trained surgeon who treats the
troubles and the diseases of the eyes. Popularly he is called
an *oculist* (OK'-yə-list), or, even more popularly, an eye
doctor.

6. The *optometrist* (op-TOM'-ə-trist) checks and cor-
rects vision, usually by prescribing and fitting eyeglasses.
He practices *optometry* (op-TOM'-ə-tree).

7. The *optician* (op-TISH'-ən) is a technician who

grinds lenses to an ophthalmologist's or optometrist's prescription or who makes or sells eyeglasses, binoculars, and other optical instruments.

8. The *gynecologist* (guy'-nə-KOL'-ə-jist; the first syllable may also be pronounced *jine* or *jin*) specializes in the diseases that are peculiar to women. His profession is *gynecology* (guy'-nə-KOL'-ə-jee). (Almost all *gynecologists* also practice *obstetrics,* as noted above.)

9. The *dermatologist* (dur'-mə-TOL'-ə-jist) specializes in diseases of the skin—rash, acne, allergies, lesions, psoriasis, eczema, etc. His specialty is *dermatology* (dur'-mə-TOL'-ə-jee).

10. The *psychiatrist* (sy-KY'-ə-trist; the first syllable may also be pronounced *sə*) is a medical specialist in mental ailments, emotional problems, psychoses, neuroses, etc. He practices *psychiatry* (sy-KY'-ə-tree).

11. The *orthodontist* (or'-thə-DON'-tist) specializes in straightening crooked teeth and in correcting bad "bites," or, as they are called in the vocabulary of *orthodontia* (or'-thə-DON'-shə), "malocclusions."

II
Which Specialist Would You Visit?

Write the title of the specialist you would suggest for each of the following ailments.

1. You have a painful corn. ....
2. You need eyeglasses. ....
3. Your baby has the colic. ....
4. You need a doctor to deliver your baby. ....
5. A friend of yours has had a complete mental collapse. ....
6. A child you know has crooked teeth. ....
7. A woman is suffering from female disorders. ....
8. You are troubled with a skin rash. ....
9. You have an eye disease that needs expert attention. ....

10. You have an illness which you believe can be cured by bone manipulation. ....

11. You want new frames for your glasses. ....

ANSWERS: (1) podiatrist *or* chiropodist; (2) optometrist; (3) pediatrician; (4) obstetrician; (5) psychiatrist; (6) orthodontist; (7) gynecologist; (8) dermatologist; (9) oculist *or* ophthalmologist; (10) osteopath; (11) optician

III
Test Your Linguistic Instinct

You have studied the titles of eleven specialists and the form that designates the profession or practice of each one. (An *obstetrician* practices *obstetrics,* a *pediatrician* is involved in *pediatrics,* etc.) Can you, now, figure out the *adjective* form of each word that would *describe* the practitioner or his work? For example, the *obstetrician* has *obstetrical* patients.

1. The *pediatrician* has .... patients.
2. The *podiatrist* has .... patients.
3. The *osteopath* engages in .... healing.
4. The *ophthalmologist* does .... work.
5. The *optometrist* has an .... practice.
6. The *gynecologist* treats .... cases.
7. The *dermatologist* treats .... conditions.
8. The *psychiatrist* handles .... problems.
9. The *orthodontist* handles .... problems.
10. The *optician* makes or sells .... goods.

ANSWERS: (1) pediAT'ric; (2) podiAT'ric; (3) osteoPATH'ic; (4) ophthalmoLOG'ical; (5) optoMET'ric; (6)– gynecoLOG'ical; (7)

dermatoLŌG′ical; (8) psychiAT′ric; (9) orthoDON′tic; (10) OP′tical

IV
Is There a Doctor in the House?

In a professional building in a large city, you see a number of medical titles on the doors as you go down the halls.

In each case, check the definition or description that fits each title. Before you look at the answers, see if you can name the professions of the two that are left.

Room One: The shingle says "John Doe, *Podiatrist*."
    a. He treats diseases of the skin.
    b. He's the man to see when you have an aching corn.
    c. He practices general medicine.

Room Two: The office of Richard Roe, *Psychiatrist*.
    a. He treats diseases of the skin.
    b. He corrects malocclusions.
    c. People who have emotional problems visit him.

Room Three: The office of George Jones, *Ophthalmologist*.
    a. He knows all about diseases of the eye and refractive errors, and may resort to surgery, if necessary, to correct eye ailments.
    b. He'll check your vision and prescribe glasses if you need them.
    c. He'll be happy to sell you any sort of optical instruments—binoculars, telescopes, microscopes.

Room Four: The office of James Brown, *Osteopath*.
    a. His specialty is the treatment of corns and bunions.
    b. Holding that diseases arise chiefly from displacement of the bones, with resultant pressure on nerves and blood vessels, he remedies

an ailment by manipulation of the affected parts.

c. He fills and extracts teeth.

Room Five: The name on this door is John Smith, *Obstetrician.*

a. He treats diseases and ailments peculiar to old age.

b. He specializes in the ills of infancy and childhood.

c. He delivers babies.

ANSWERS: (1) b;   (a) is a dermatologist, (c) a doctor, physician, or general practitioner;   (2) c;   (a) is a dermatologist, (b) an orthodontist;   (3) a;   (b) is an optometrist, (c) an optician;   (4) b;   (a) is a podiatrist or chiropodist, (c) a dentist;   (5) c;   (a) is a geriatrician, (b) a pediatrician.

X	X	X	X	X	X	7
8	9	10	11	12	13	14
15	16	17	18	19	20	21
22	23	24	25	26	27	28
29	30					

Verbs Give You Power

Do you remember your old schoolbook definition of a verb? It went something like this: "A verb is that part of speech which asserts, declares or predicates."

But a dynamic verb is more than this. It is the catalyst of the sentence. It is the word that brings the sentence to life.

Choose your verbs with care.

If you pick a dull verb, your speech will be dull, barely serving its primary purpose of communication, making little impression on the mind of your reader or listener.

A choice of powerful verbs, on the other hand, will make your speech electric, galvanic. Like a powder charge, it can give the impact of bullets to all the other words in your sentence.

A single illustration of this statement will be enough. Which of the two following sentences has the greater force?

1. He is a moral leper; let us keep away from him and have nothing to do with him.

2. He is a moral leper; let us *ostracize* him.

The answer is obvious, isn't it? One word has expressed the meaning of ten.

So watch your verbs. They are packed with power.

I

Here are ten dynamic verbs that belong in a rich vocabulary. We are not going to give you their precise definitions. Just read the sentences in which they occur and see if you can guess the meanings of the ones you don't already know. Pronounce them aloud.

What are some of the things people do?

1. They *expiate* (EKS'-pee-ate) their sins, crimes, blunders, or errors.
2. They *importune* (im-pər-TOON') God for divine favors.
3. They *impute* (im-PYOOT') unworthy motives to their enemies.
4. They *scintillate* (SIN'-tə-late), the wittier ones, at cocktail parties.
5. They *mulct* (MULKT) the unwary or gullible public.
6. They *ostracize* (OS'-trə-size) members of religious, political, or racial minorities.
7. They *deprecate* (DEP'-rə-kate) the foibles of others.
8. They *procrastinate* (prō-KRAS'-tə-nate) and then vow to be more punctual in the future.
9. They *rusticate* (RUSS'-tə-kate) in the summer time, if finances permit.
10. They *vegetate* (VEJ'-ə-tate) all year, if they are lacking in imagination, initiative, or energy.

II

Referring to Section I, write the proper verb next to its definition. The definitions do not appear in the same order as the sentences above.

1. Live in a passive way ....
2. Deprive of a possession unjustly ....
3. Make amends for ....
4. Beg for ceaselessly; beseech; entreat ....
5. Exclude from public or private favor; ban ....
6. Put off until a future time; delay ....
7. Sparkle with wit or humor ....
8. Spend time in the country ....
9. Ascribe, attribute, or charge an act or thought (to someone), usually in a bad or accusatory sense ....
10. Disapprove of (the actions of someone) ....

ANSWERS: (1) vegetate; (2) mulct; (3) expiate; (4) importune; (5) ostracize; (6) procrastinate; (7) scintillate; (8) rusticate; (9) impute; (10) deprecate

III

Which of the verbs most aptly describes the characteristic action of the following people?

1. He is too indolent to get his work done on time   He ....
2. He is accustomed to blaming others.   He ....
3. He is a sparkling and witty person.   He ....
4. He is remorseful and wishes to make amends.   He ....
5. He is a person who is in a rut and leads a monotonous life.   He ....

6. He is an exclusive individual, avoiding people who are different from himself.   He ....
7. He cheats others.   He ....
8. He's an insistent beggar.   He ....
9. He looks down on the acts of others.   He ....
10. He is on a vacation in the country.   He ....

ANSWERS: (1) procrastinates; (2) imputes; (3) scintillates; (4) expiates; (5) vegetates; (6) ostracizes; (7) mulcts; (8) importunes; (9) deprecates; (10) rusticates

IV

You will find, below, eleven pairs of sentences. The second sentence of each pair has a blank line that corresponds to an italicized phrase in the first sentence. Write, on this blank line, either another form of, or a noun or adjective derived from, one of the verbs we have studied in this chapter.

1. He has been *spending his time in the country*. He has been ....
2. Why do you keep *nagging me for favors?* Why are you so ....?
3. He took $1,000,000 from the public *by dishonest methods*. He .... the public of $1,000,000.
4. *Excluding him from our group* is our most potent weapon against someone who is disloyal. .... is our most potent weapon against someone who is disloyal.
5. For the past two years, I have been *accomplishing nothing and getting nowhere*. For the past two years, I have been ....

6. He *showed contempt and disapproval of* the younger generation. He .... the younger generation.

7. *To make amends for* his sin, he did penance for three days. In .... of his sin, he did penance for three days.

8. Do they *accuse* me *of committing* these offenses? Have they .... these offenses to me?

9. I resent your *accusation that* I *committed these offenses*. I resent your .... of these offenses to me.

10. She is a *sparkling and witty* speaker. She is a .... speaker.

11. *Putting off till tomorrow* is the thief of time. .... is the thief of time.

ANSWERS: (1) rusticating; (2) importunate; (3) mulcted; (4) ostracism; (5) vegetating; (6) deprecated; (7) expiation; (8) imputed; (9) imputation; (10) scintillating; (11) procrastination

V

Now for a change of pace, with a few verbal gymnastics for you. Can you think of five verbs ending in *ate?* They have not appeared in this chapter. The definitions and initial letters are offered to help you.

1. Have control over   D ....
2. Make easier   F ....
3. Follow the example of   E ....
4. Make gestures or motions to convey meanings   G ....
5. Get better   R ....

ANSWERS: (1) dominate (DOM′-ə-nate); (2) facilitate (fə-SIL′-ə-tate); (3) emulate (EM′-yə-late);

(4) gesticulate (jess-TIK'-yə-late); (5) recuperate (ree-KŌŌ'-pə-rate)

Now can you think of five verbs ending in *ize?*

1. Be condescending toward   P ....
2. Make pay a fine or suffer punish-   P ....
   ment
3. Make vivid or moving   D ....
4. Make live forever   I ....
5. Appropriate and claim as one's
   own the literary work of another   P ....

ANSWERS: (1) patronize (PAT'-rə-nize); (2) penalize
         (PEE'-nə-lize); (3) dramatize (DRAM'-ə-
         tize); (4) immortalize (i-MORE'-tə-lize);
         (5) plagiarize (PLAY'-jee-ə-rise)

VI

Can you make the verbs of Section V an active part of
your speaking vocabulary? Fill the blanks of the following
sentences. Some new form of the verb may be required,
such as *dominates, dominating, dominated.*

1. Beethoven's compositions have always ....
   the musical scene.
2. Carl Sandburg's biography vividly ....
   the life of Lincoln as no other book has ever been
   able to.
3. I have never seen a sick man .... so
   quickly.
4. Your friends think you are conceited because you
   seem to .... them.
5. Nature will .... you for your alcoholic
   excesses.
6. Let us .... the habits of successful
   men.
7. In her confusion, she .... wildly.

8. He built an insecure and dishonest literary reputation by .... the classics.
9. Let me pack for you; that will .... your departure.
10. The "Elegy in a Country Churchyard" did much to .... the poet Thomas Gray.

ANSWERS: (1) dominated; (2) dramatizes; (3) recuperate; (4) patronize; (5) penalize; (6) emulate; (7) gesticulated; (8) plagiarizing; (9) facilitate; (10) immortalize

VII

Twenty dynamic verbs, excellent additions to a powerful vocabulary, have been discussed in this chapter. How many of them can you call to mind? Let us put your learning and retention to a test.

In order to prompt your memory, the initial letters are given. Recall and write down as many as you can before referring to the preceding pages to check yourself. A score of twelve out of twenty is fair, fifteen good, eighteen or nineteen excellent, all twenty superb.

1. E	11. D ....
2. I	12. F ....
3. I	13. E ....
4. S	14. G ....
5. M	15. R ....
6. O	16. P ....
7. D	17. P ....
8. P	18. D ....
9. R	19. I ....
10. V	20. P ....

For the next few days keep your eyes and ears alert for verbs. Note them as you read, or as people speak to you. See whether they are effective and do their work. Billboards, car-cards, and other advertisements will be par-

ticularly helpful, for advertising space costs money and the
publicity men have to pick their verbs with care. As you
read your newspaper, watch for examples of well-chosen,
dynamic verbs.

Take care of your verbs. They will add power, color,
and punch to your speech and writing.

X	X	X	X	X	X	X
8	9	10	11	12	13	14
15	16	17	18	19	20	21
22	23	24	25	26	27	28
29	30					

Words About
Theories

The mentally alert person is not content to live merely from day to day, completely circumscribed by such things as food, money, clothing, and entertainment. Occasionally he is tempted to speculate on *why* he is living and what the controlling forces of his life are. This chapter deals with a few of the terms that are applied to these motivating forces by different people who have varying points of view.

1. Is there a God? Nothing so closely approaches the outer limits of abstraction as theorizing about a supernatural and supreme being. Many of us worship, most of us at least accept, some form of deity. Do you belong to the minority who insist, often belligerently, that man makes God in his own image, that God is a figment of the imagination and hence completely, irrevocably nonexistent? Then you are an *atheist* (AY′-thee-ist; *th* as in *think*) and your philosophy is called *atheism* (AY′-thee-iz-əm).

The word is from the Greek *a,* "without," and *theos,* "god."

2. To many other thinkers it seems more reasonable to say that the existence or nonexistence of a supreme being is one mystery the human mind will never fathom. How did the world come into being? How did life begin? Is there a father who looks after his children, or are we the products of purposeless chance? Do you answer these questions by saying that no one knows and no one can ever hope to know? Then you are an *agnostic* (ag-NOSS'-tik), and your doctrine is called *agnosticism* (ag-NOSS'-tə-siz-əm). This word, too, is from the Greek, derived from *agnostos,* "not knowing."

3. Why did that young child dart across the roadway just as a huge truck rounded the bend? How do you explain the needless snuffing out of an innocent life? Is it due to blind chance? To cause and effect? Why should some great benefactor of humanity be cut off in his prime? Are such events controlled by accident? Or are they determined by fate? (*Fate,* incidentally, is derived from the Latin *fatus,* "spoken" or "predicted.")

If you believe that everything that happens is predetermined, foreordained, written down, as it were, on the far-off pages of some mighty volume, you are a *fatalist* (FAY'-tə-list) and your theory is called *fatalism* (FAY'-tə-liz-əm).

4. In this world of ours you will find some people who think only of themselves and of their own selfish advantage, and who actually maintain that all virtue consists in the pursuit of self-interest. Completely indifferent to the needs, feelings, or wishes of others, they base their actions on personal gain and direct benefit. They believe in, and are motivated by, *egoism* (EE'-gō-iz-əm); a member of such a cult is an *egoist* (EE'-gō-ist). (These words, characteristically, derive from the Latin *ego,* "I.")

5. If your characteristics are opposite to those of an egoist, if you have an unselfish regard for, and devotion to, the interests and needs of others, then you are an *altruist* (AL'-trōō-ist) and you practice *altruism* (AL'trōō-iz-əm).

The relationship of this word to the Latin *alter,* "other," is clear.

6. Can you rise above petty considerations of pleasure and pain, joy and grief? Can you meet adversity with indifference and submit to the arrows and slings of misfortune with a dignified resignation? Can you give up envy, greed, jealousy, hatred, and other human passions? Can you suffer mental and physical pain without complaint? If you can honestly say "yes" to these questions, and if you sincerely believe that such self-control makes for a better way of life, then you are a *stoic* (STŌ'ik), a practitioner of *stoicism* (STŌ'-ə-siz-əm). The founder of *stoicism* was the Greek philosopher Zeno, who lived about three hundred years before Christ. *Stoic* is from the Greek *stoikos,* which, in turn, is from *stoa,* "porch." Zeno taught in the Stoa Poikile, or "Painted Porch," in Athens.

7. Are you apt to say: "No other nation can hold a candle to my country. We are the supermen, the chosen people. Every other race is inferior to mine and they are all destined to be our slaves when the day comes"? This is not patriotism. Or, rather, it is patriotism carried to an illogical and ludicrous extreme. If you happen to talk this way, you are a *chauvinist* (SHŌ'-və-nist); you are addicted to *chauvinism* (SHŌ'-və-niz-əm). These terms come from the name of a real man, Nicolas Chauvin of Rochefort, who was so demonstrative in his devotion to Napoleon and to the imperial cause that he was ridiculed on the French stage at the time.

8. Are you a braggart about your country's power? Do you always want your nation to use force? Do you want to call out the Army, Navy, and Air Force on the slightest provocation, and send our soldiers and sailors around the world to show those "damn foreigners" who's the boss? "Do the other nations want war?" you ask. "We'll give it to them. And if they don't want it, we'll give it to them anyway." If this is a description of your philosophy, you are a *jingoist* (JING'-gō-ist), and your heart beats in tune with the martial music of *jingoism* (JING'-gō-iz-əm). (The "Jingoes" were originally a section of the Conservative

party in England in 1877 who were eager to have their nation support the Turks in the Russo-Turkish war.)

9. Is it best that our government follow the political faith, methods, and tenets of our fathers and grandfathers, or shall we move rapidly ahead, change constantly, explore and experiment? Those who believe in *liberalism* follow the latter philosophy. They owe allegiance to no party, are independent in thought and action, and are always anathema to those who wish the government to pursue the well-trodden paths. *Liberals* prefer a changing, dynamic, experimenting government. They vote for progress, sometimes in the sense that anything new and different and previously untried is progressive. The Romans gave us the word *liber,* "free."

10. The *conservative,* on the other hand, is opposed to change. He believes that what is, is best. He prefers that his government follow familiar, tried, tested, and safe policies. "We're content with what we have," he says. "Why take the risk of sailing into uncharted waters?" The word derives from Latin *conservare,* "to preserve." (An extreme *liberal* is a *radical;* an extreme *conservative* is a *reactionary.*)

11. What type of life is best? To one group of thinkers, such a question has a simple answer. That life is the most successful, says the *epicurean* (ep'-ə-kyŏŏ-REE'-ən), which brings to each person the maximum of pleasure and the minimum of pain. The doctrine of *epicureanism* (ep'-ə-kyŏŏ-REE'-ə-niz-əm) teaches that pleasure is the chief good. (*Epicurean* should not be confused with *epicure,* one who enjoys the delights of the table and who is expert and fastidious in his choice of food.)

Ready for a check on your learning and retention?

I

What philosophy is expressed by each of the statements below?

1. "I'm interested in the welfare of the other fellow, not in my own."

   A ....

2. "Let the other fellow take care of himself. My interests come first, last, and always."

   E ....

3. "Mine is the superior race. Have we not the monopoly on beauty, strength, brains, creativeness, honesty, virtue, and bravery?"

   C ....

4. "Let's not stand still in politics. Progress, change, experimentation—that's what we need!"

   L ....

5. "Happiness, pleasure, fun, revelry: these are the most important things in life."

   E ....

6. "There's a God? Don't be silly. Only stupid people believe in God."

   A ....

7. "Maybe there is a God. Maybe there isn't. I don't know, and I don't believe anybody else does or ever will."

   A ....

8. "The wise and brave man is indifferent to both pain and pleasure."

   S ....

9. "We'll build up our nuclear power, our troops, and our navy; we'll arm to the hilt. Then we'll dare any nation in the world to knock the chip off our shoulder!"

   J ....

10. "You can't change the future. It's all planned and written down."

    F ....

11. "Let's keep things just as they are. We're getting along all right, so why fool around with any dangerous half-baked, new-fangled theories?"

    C ....

ANSWERS: (1) altruist; (2) egoist; (3) chauvinist; (4) liberal; (5) epicurean; (6) atheist; (7) agnostic; (8) stoic; (9) jingoist; (10) fatalist; (11) conservative

II

Adjective forms of these nouns are as follows:

NOUN	ADJECTIVE
altruism	*altruistic*
atheism	*atheistic*
agnosticism	*agnostic*
fatalism	*fatalistic*
egoism	*egoistic*
stoicism	*stoical*
chauvinism	*chauvinistic*
jingoism	*jingoistic*
liberalism	*liberal*
conservatism	*conservative*
epicureanism	*epicurean*

Can you fit the correct adjective in each of the following phrases or sentences?

1. The .... attitude of the ungodly.
2. The .... doubts of the skeptical.
3. Age tends to bring a .... tinge to one's politics.
4. Politically, youth is inclined to be..........................
5. The .... flavor of oriental religions.
6. The narrow, ... desires of the conceited.
7. The .... resignation of those who have suffered much.
8. The .... blatancy of professional "flag-wavers."
9. The .... desires of the self-indulgent.
10. Threats, "saber-rattling," and a call-up of the reserves have often been the .... means by which strong nations have imposed their will on their weaker neighbors.
11. The .... attitudes of most parents to their children.

v

ANSWERS: (1) atheistic; (2) agnostic; (3) conservative; (4) liberal; (5) fatalistic; (6) ego-
istic; (7) stoical; (8) chauvinistic; (9)
epicurean; (10) jingoistic; (11) altruistic

III

Finally, to make these words an integral part of your
thinking and speaking vocabulary, try this exercise. Can
you react immediately to each statement as either essentially *true* or generally *false*? Read each statement quickly,
once only, then check at once the answer you trust.

1. The *altruist* hates people.   True...... False......
2. An *atheist* is a steady church-
   goer.   True...... False......
3. The *agnostic* is deeply religious.   True...... False......
4. A *fatalist* never takes chances.   True...... False......
5. An *egoist* wants to help his fel-
   low-man.   True...... False......
6. The *stoic* becomes hysterical
   under the stress of tragedy or
   disaster.   True...... False......
7. *Chauvinists* often switch their
   allegiance to other nations.   True...... False......
8. A *jingoist* is interested in peace
   at any cost.   True...... False......
9. A political *liberal* shies away
   from innovation.   True...... False......
10. A political *conservative* be-
    lieves in greatly enhanced Fed-
    eral power.   True...... False......
11. An *epicurean* pursues a life of
    austerity and self-denial.   True...... False......

ANSWERS: All statements, of course, are outrageously
false.

X̶1̶	X̶2̶	X̶3̶	X̶4̶	X̶5̶	X̶6̶	X̶7̶
X̶8̶	9	10	11	12	13	14
15	16	17	18	19	20	21
22	23	24	25	26	27	28
29	30					

Quick Vocabulary Builder

English is a reservoir of the classical languages. It has taken over to itself and has absorbed for its own use more than 25 per cent of the Greek language and more than 50 per cent of the Latin language. It is obvious, then, that a knowledge of Greek and Latin roots is invaluable in any program of vocabulary building.

In the exercises ahead we will take English words apart and will show how you can easily identify and understand scores of words that you may never have seen before.

I

1. *Monogamy* (mə-NOG′-ə-mee). A one-to-one system of marriage; a man or woman has only one current spouse at any time. From Greek *monos,* "one," *gamos,* "marriage."

2. *Bigamy* (BIG′-ə-mee). Illegal involvement by one

person in two or more concurrent marriages. From Latin *bis*, "twice" or "two," plus *gamos*.

3. *Polygamy* (pə-LIG'-ə-mee). A custom, once prevalent among the Mormons in Utah and encountered today in some parts of Asia, Africa, the Near East, etc., in which a man has more than one wife. The first part of the word is from Greek *polys*, "many."

4. *Misogamy* (mə-SOG'-ə-mee). Hatred of marriage. From Greek *misein*, "to hate," plus *gamos*.

II

Notice how the Greek and Latin roots discussed in the previous section lead to four new words.

1. *Monotheism* (MON'-ə-thee-iz'-əm). The belief in a single, supreme deity. Greek *monos*, "one," combined with *theos*, "god."

2. *Bicuspid* (by-KUS'-pid). A tooth with two prongs. Latin *bis*, "twice" or "two," and *cuspis*, "point."

3. *Polyglot* (POL'-ee-glot'). *Glotta* is Greek for "tongue"; the *polyglot* is one who speaks many tongues or languages.

4. *Misanthropy* (mə-SAN'-thrə-pee). *Anthropos* is Greek for "man." We have, then, the hatred of man or of mankind. A *misanthrope* (MISS'-ən-thrope), therefore, is anyone who has a morbid aversion to, or distrust of, his fellow men.

III

Let us take a quick review of the roots we've discovered so far. Can you remember the meaning of each word using these roots?

1. *Monos* (Greek), "one," as in *monogamy* and *monotheism*

2. *Gamos* (Greek), "marriage," as in *monogamy, bigamy, misogamy,* and *polygamy*

3. *Bis* (Latin), "twice" or "two," as in *bigamy* and *bicuspid*

4. *Polys* (Greek), "many," as in *polygamy* and *polyglot*

5. *Misein* (Greek), "to hate," as in *misogamy* and *misanthropy*

6. *Theos* (Greek), "god," as in *monotheism, bitheism,* and *polytheism*

7. *Cuspis* (Latin), "point," as in *bicuspid*

8. *Glotta* (Greek), "tongue," as in *polyglot*

9. *Anthropos* (Greek), "man," as in *misanthropy*

IV

Now on to further explorations into roots:

1. *Theology* (thee-OL'-ə-jee). The study of God and religion. To *theos* we add the Greek root *logos,* "knowledge," "study," or "word."

2. *Philanthropy* (fə-LAN'-thrə-pee). Love of mankind. The root *anthropos* is combined with the Greek *philein,* "to love." A *philanthropist* (fə-LAN'-thrə-pist), then, who gives money to the poor, is literally a "lover of his fellowmen."

3. *Anthropology* (an'-thrō-POL'-ə-jee). Study of man, i.e., science of human development and history—a combination of *anthropos* and *logos.*

4. *Philology* (fe-LOL'-ə-jee). Study of language, i.e., science of linguistics—literally, a love of words, from *philein* combined with *logos.*

V

Ready for a test of your knowledge of Greek and Latin roots? Write the meaning of each root in the appropriate blank below, then give one example of an English word based on this root.

ROOT	MEANING	EXAMPLE
1. *bis*	....	....
2. *theos*	....	....
3. *philein*	....	....
4. *misein*	....	....
5. *gamos*	....	....
6. *glotta*	....	....
7. *monos*	....	....
8. *cuspis*	....	....
9. *polys*	....	....
10. *anthropos*	....	....
11. *logos*	....	....

ANSWERS: (1) twice, two; (2) god; (3) love; (4) hate; (5) marriage; (6) tongue; (7) one; (8) point; (9) many; (10) man, mankind; (11) study, knowledge, word

To check your examples, refer to previous pages.

VI

Can you qualify as a word detective? Keep in mind the eleven roots we have discussed and try to arrive at the meanings of the italicized words. Guess intelligently, referring to previous explanations as often as you wish to. Write your meaning in the blank line following each sentence.

1. Some Englishmen wear a *monocle* (MON'-ə-kəl).

....

2. He delivered an interesting *monologue* (MON'-ə-log').

....

3. He has a *monopoly* of the coffee market (mə-NOP'-ə-lee).

4. He lives in a *monastery* (MON'-ə-stair'-ee).

5. He is riding a *bicycle* (BY'-sə-kol).

6. Man is a *biped* (BY'-ped).

7. France and England made a *bilateral* (by-LAT'-ə-rəl) agreement.

8. A rectangle is a *polygon* (POL'-ee-gon').

9. A *misogynist* (mə-SAHJ'-ə-nist) shuns the company of women.

10. Romans practiced *polytheism* (POL'-ee-thee-iz'-əm).

11. This tooth is a *tricuspid* (try-KUS'-pid).

12. The President's wonderful stamp collection is the envy of *philatelists* (fə-LAT'-ə-lists).

13. The *anthropoid* (AN'-thrə-poid') apes are similar in appearance to humans.

14. *Biology* (by-OL'-ə-jee) is a fascinating science.

....

15. England is a *monarchy* (MON'-ər-kee).

....

ANSWERS: (1) lens for *one* eye; (2) speech by *one* person; (3) control by *one* person (of the market); (4) place where people live *alone;* (5) vehicle of *two* wheels; (6) creature with *two* feet; (7) *two*-sided; (8) *many*-sided figure; (9) *hater* of women; (10) belief in *many* gods; (11) tooth with three *points;* (12) *lovers,* hence collectors, of stamps; (13) *man*like; (14) *study* of life; (15) country where *one* person rules

VII

Consider, perhaps with amazement, how many new words you have learned in a very short time by tracing them back to their Latin or Greek derivation. Pronounce each aloud as you come to it, and review briefly its meaning as reflected by the root structure.

1. *gamos,* marriage
   monogamy (mə-NOG'-ə-mee)
   bigamy (BIG'-ə-mee)
   polygamy (pə-LIG'-ə-mee)
   misogamy (mə-SOG'-ə-mee)

2. *monos,* one
   monotheism (MON'-ə-thee-iz'-əm)
   monogamy (mə-NOG'-ə-mee)
   monocle (MON'-ə-kəl)
   monologue (MON'-ə-log')
   monopoly (mə-NOP'-ə-lee)
   monastery (MON'-ə-stair'-ee)
   monarchy (MON'-ər-kee)

3. *bis*, twice, two
   bicuspid (by-KUS'-pid)
   bicycle (BY'-sə-kol)
   biped (BY'-ped)
   bilateral (by-LAT'-ə-rəl)
   bigamous (BIG'-ə-məs)

4. *polys*, many
   polygamy (pə-LIG'-ə-mee)
   polyglot (POL'-ee-glot')
   polygon (POL'-ee-gon')
   polytheism (POL'-ee-thee-iz'-əm)

5. *misein*, to hate
   misogamy (mə-SOG'-ə-mee)
   misogynist (mə-SAHJ'-ə-nist)
   misanthropy (mə-SAN'-thrə-pee)

6. *theos*, god
   theology (thee-OL'-ə-jee)
   monotheist (MON'-ə-thee-ist)

7. *logos*, word, study, knowledge
   biology (by-OL'-ə-jee)
   theology (thee-OL'-ə-jee)
   philology (fə-LOL'-ə-jee)
   anthropology (an'-thrō-POL'-ə-jee)

8. *philein*, to love
   philologist (fə-LOL'-ə-jist)
   philatelist (fə-LAT'-ə-list)
   philanthropy (fə-LAN'-thrə-pee)

9. *anthropos*, man, mankind
   anthropoid (AN'-thrə-poid)
   anthropologist (an-thrə-POL'-ə-jist)
   philanthropist (fə-LAN'-thrə-pist)
   misanthrope (MISS'-ən-thrope)
   misanthropist (mis-AN'-thrə-pist)

10. *cuspis*, point
    bicuspid (by-KUS'-pid)
    tricuspid (try-KUS'-pid)

11. *glotta*, tongue
    polyglot (POL'-ee-glot')

VIII

Final review time! If you feel a happy and secure control of the material of this chapter, try this simple test, in which you have to fill in one or more blanks in each sentence. Can you make a perfect score without referring to previous information?

1. One who practices *monogamy* has only one
   ....
2. A *misogamist* .... marriage.
3. *Theology* is the study of .... or ....
4. *Biology* is the .... of life.
5. A *philatelist* collects ....
6. A *misanthropist* .... mankind.
7. *Anthropology* is the science of .... development.
8. A *bicuspid* has .... points.
9. A *tricuspid* has .... points.
10. *Anthropoid* means "similar to, or in the form of, a .... "
11. A *polyglot* speaks .... languages.
12. A *polygon* has .... sides.
13. Under *polygamy,* a man may have .... wives.
14. In America, a *bigamous* marriage is ....
15. In a *monotheistic* religion, there is only one
    ....
16. A *biped* has two ....
17. A two-wheeled vehicle is a ....
18. An agreement endorsed by two sides is called
    ....
19. A lens for only one eye is called a ....
20. A speech by one person is a ....
21. Control of the market by one person or group is a ....
22. A place where men live in seclusion is a ....

23. A nation which has one, usually hereditary, ruler
    is a ....

24. Belief in many gods is called ....

25. A *misogynist* hates ....

ANSWERS: (1) spouse, wife, husband;   (2) hates;   (3)
         God, religion;   (4) study, science;   (5)
         stamps;   (6) hates;   (7) human, man's,
         mankind's;   (8) two;   (9) three;   (10)
         human, human being, man, person, etc.;   (11)
         many;   (12) many;   (13) many;   (14) il-
         legal, unlawful, etc.;   (15) God;   (16) legs,
         feet;   (17) bicycle;   (18) bilateral;   (19)
         monocle;   (20) monologue;   (21) monopo-
         ly;   (22) monastery;   (23) monarchy;
         (24) polytheism;   (25) women, females, etc.

~~1~~	~~2~~	3	~~4~~	~~5~~	~~6~~	~~7~~
~~8~~	~~9~~	10	11	12	13	14
15	16	17	18	19	20	21
22	23	24	25	26	27	28
29	30					

A Quick Test of Your Progress to Date

You are of course aware that you will never add very rapidly to your vocabulary by merely being *exposed* to words, or by reading, or by talking. *You must have a plan.*

Here is one way to get ahead with words in everyday life. It's the simplest thing in the world.

Buy a small pocket notebook. When you read a newspaper, a magazine, or a book, or listen to TV or the radio, and come upon a strange word, enter it in your notebook. Then look it up in the dictionary. If you find that it's some abstruse or highly technical term, such as, say, *syzygy,* "an immovable union between two brachials of a crinoid," just pass it by. You won't be using it unless you are studying to be a professor of biology. But if it sounds like a word that will be helpful to you, take possession of it, make it your own personal property. Say it aloud many times. Study its definition, note its derivation. Be sure, also, to copy from the dictionary the sample sentence in which it is used, if such is given. Then write your own sentence along the lines of the example in the dictionary.

All this will take only a few minutes or so, but it is necessary to make the practice a daily habit. Then the list in your notebook will grow and grow, as will your command of English.

We want, at this point, to help you gain complete possession of any of the words in the first eight chapters that may have once been unfamiliar to you.

In this review, you have, as usual, the responsibility of grading yourself. After you have compared your answers with those given at the end of the chapter, we will give you an interpretation of your score and you can then see what progress you have made.

I

1. The study of the origins of words or of word histories is called
   (a) philology; (b) verbology; (c) etymology
2. The "taxicabs" in Ancient Rome gave rise to our word
   (a) calculate; (b) supercilious; (c) captain
3. The Greek syllable *graph* means
   (a) seeing; (b) writing; (c) speaking
4. The word *run* has approximately .... different dictionary meanings.
   (a) 3; (b) 20; (c) 90
5. Some words require emotional maturity to be understood.
   (a) True? *or* (b) False?

II

Each phrase in column B defines a word in column A. Match the two columns.

A	B
1. *vicarious*	a. appeal to the baser emotions
2. *rationalize*	b. tearfully sentimental
3. *gregarious*	c. company-loving
4. *obsequious*	d. second-hand or substitutional in experience
5. *maudlin*	e. fawning and servile
6. *ascetic*	f. justify, usually unconsciously (an unworthy act)
7. *pander*	g. severely self-denying
8. *sublimate*	h. refine; turn into higher or socially acceptable channels
9. *wanton*	i. worn out; sterile; exhausted from rich or overindulgent living
10. *effete*	j. unrestrained

III

Check the correct forms:

1. The *obstetrician:*
   (a) delivers babies; (b) treats babies; (c) treats women's diseases
2. The *osteopath:*
   (a) straightens teeth; (b) specializes in skin diseases; (c) treats diseases by manipulating the bones
3. The *optometrist:*
   (a) sells lenses; (b) measures your eyes for glasses; (c) operates on your eyes
4. The *podiatrist:*
   (a) treats foot ailments; (b) treats mental ailments; (c) treats nerve ailments
5. The *psychiatrist* is interested in:
   (a) your stomach; (b) your mind; (c) your eyes

IV

Write the required verb:

1. To stagnate   V ....
2. To postpone   P ....
3. To cheat; to deprive fraudulently   M ....
4. To exclude; to ban   O ....
5. To atone for   E ....
6. To entreat   I ....
7. To sparkle   S ....
8. To disapprove of   D ....
9. To spend time in the country   R ....
10. To charge (someone with)   I ....

V

Fill in each blank space with the type of person who would be most apt to make such a statement.

1. "I have good taste in foods and
   wines."   E ....
2. "Government should experiment."   L ....
3. "Government must not experi-
   ment."   C ....
4. "If they don't want war, give it
   to them anyway."   J ....
5. "My country is the only one
   worth anything."   CH ....
6. "Pain will never make me
   wince."   S ....
7. "The other fellow comes first."   A ....
8. "I come first above all."   E ....
9. "There is no God."   A ....
10. "I don't know whether or not
    there is a God."   A ....
11. "Everything will happen as it will,
    no matter what we do."   F ....

VI

Give the meaning of each of the following Greek or Latin roots:

1. *logos*   ....
2. *theos*   ....
3. *bis*   ....
4. *philein*   ....
5. *misein*   ....
6. *monos*   ....
7. *anthropos* ....
8. *polys*   ....
9. *gamos*   ....
10. *cuspis*   ....
11. *glotta*   ....

ANSWERS: I: (1) c;   (2) a;   (3) b;   (4) c;
          (5) a
          Scoring: Two points each
                        Your Score: ....

         II: (1) d;   (2) f;   (3) c;   (4) e;
          (5) b;   (6) g;   (7) a;   (8) h;
          (9) j;   (10) i
          Scoring: Two points each
                        Your Score: ....

        III: (1) a;   (2) c;   (3) b;   (4) a;
          (5) b
          Scoring: Two points each
                        Your Score: ....

         IV: (1) vegetate;   (2) procrastinate;
          (3) mulct;   (4) ostracize;   (5)
          expiate;   (6) importune;   (7)
          scintillate;   (8) deprecate;   (9)
          rusticate;   (10) impute
          Scoring: Two points each
                        Your Score: ....

          V: (1) epicure;   (2) liberal;   (3)
          conservative;   (4) jingoist;   (5)

chauvinist; (6) stoic; (7) altruist; (8) egoist; (9) atheist;
(10) agnostic; (11) fatalist
Scoring: Two points each
Your Score: ....
VI: (1)   word,   knowledge,   study;
(2) god; (3) twice, two; (4)
love; (5) hate; (6) one; (7)
man, mankind; (8) many; (9)
marriage; (10) point; (11)
tongue
Scoring: Two points each
Your Score: ....

Maximum Score: 104
Your Total Score: ....

What Your Score Means

58 or under suggests the possibility that you may
not be thorough enough as you go along. Work
harder; review more frequently! Try to improve
your score on the next general test of your progress.

60–70 is an average and acceptable score. Can you do
still better next time?

72–86 shows better-than-average learning. Continue
building your word power and no doors will ever
be closed to you. Can you, nevertheless, improve
your score next time?

88–104 indicates remarkable progress. Your interest and
self-motivation are high, and your rewards from
this work will therefore be great.

Words About
Your Fellow Men

We have now a wide and most important group of words to consider. These are the words that describe and catalog a few of the various classes of our fellowmen and that identify some of their activities. And here is a helpful game that you might like to try. Just jot down on the margin of these pages, opposite each of the twenty-five words that follow, the name of a friend of yours or a well-known actor or public character who, you believe, would best personify the particular word under discussion. Dramatizing the word in this fashion will help fix its meaning in your mind.

You will meet some familiar words in this list, words that we have introduced in previous chapters. But repetition is a part of learning, and very often, when a word appears a second time, it will be presented in another form and with a considerably enriched meaning.

Let us look over a few of the words that characterize the varied types of personalities who inhabit our interesting world.

I

1. The *coquette* (kō-KET'). This girl promises much, flirts egregiously, and delivers very little.
2. The *circe* (SUR'-see). Her greatest pleasure comes from luring men to their destruction.
3. The *amazon* (AM'-ə-zon'). She's the tall, strapping, masculine kind of woman.
4. The *virago* (və-RAY'-gō). She is the loud-mouthed, turbulent, battle-axe type; a vicious nag and scold.
5. The *adonis* (ə-DON'-əs). He's the handsome, Greek-god type who makes the hearts of young girls flutter.

II

1. The *judas* (JOO'-dəs). Don't trust him. He's the traitor who will sell out his best friend for money.
2. The *futilitarian* (fyoo-til'-ə-TAIR'-ee-ən). The pessimist and cynic who sees no particular point to anything in life.
3. The *vulgarian* (vul-GAIR'-ee-ən). He has vulgar tastes and manners.
4. The *pedant* (PED'-ənt). His greatest delight is making an unnecessary show of his learning, especially by correcting petty errors. He attaches exaggerated importance to minute and minor details of scholarship.
5. The *egoist* (EE'-gō-ist.) His credo is selfishness. His interests come first, and no one else matters.
6. The *ascetic* (a-SET'-ik). He lives a severely temperate life and avoids human pleasures and vices.
7. The *esthete* (ESS'-theet). He is a person of fine taste and artistic flair. Hence, he is most responsive to, and delighted with, whatever is beautiful.

III

1. The *demagogue* (DEM'-ə-gog'). By appealing to the prejudices and hatreds of the population, he foments social discontent in order to further his own political ambitions.
2. The *martinet* (mar'-tə-NET'). He's fanatic in his insistence on blind discipline from his subordinates, and a tiresome stickler for form and etiquette.
3. The *sycophant* (SIK'-ə-fənt). By insincere flattery and pretended servility, he hopes to make rich or influential people think of him kindly, especially when they have some crumbs to throw.

IV

1. The *atheist* (AY'-thee-ist). He's sure God is non-existent.
2. The *agnostic* (ag-NOSS'-tik). He maintains that the human mind is incapable of penetrating the mystery of divine existence. Perhaps there is a God, perhaps not. No man knows.

V

1. The *tyro* (TY'-rō). He's a beginner in some profession, occupation, or art.
2. The *virtuoso* (vur'-choo-O'-sō). He is the antithesis of the tyro, having reached the greatest heights of skill and competence in music, painting, or any one of the fine arts.
3. The *philologist* (fə-LOL'-ə-jist). He's a scholar of language and speech.
4. The *clairvoyant* (klair-VOY'-ənt). He claims the ability to see things not visible to those with normal

sight. Hence, he often makes prophecies about the future.

VI

1. The *philatelist* (fə-LAT'-ə-list). He's the stamp collector.
2. The *numismatist* (nōō'-MIZ'-mə-tist). He's the coin collector.

VII

1. The *gourmet* (gōōr-MAY'). He is knowledgeable and fastidious about eating and drinking, devoting himself to excellent food, special wines, exotic seasonings, etc.
2. The *connoisseur* (kon'-ə-SUR'). He is a critical judge of excellence in the arts, food, drink, women, etc.

VIII
Test Your Learning

Can you fill the blank line with the word that fits each description?

1. He does not believe in God.   A ....
2. He is a skillful practitioner of some art.   V ....
3. He collects rare coins.   N ....
4. He has an unusual appreciation of beauty.   E ....
5. He is ostentatious about his learning.   P ....
6. He will betray a friend.   J ....
7. She is a flirt.   C ....
8. She is a destructive siren.   C ....

9. He is an offensive stickler for discipline.   M ....
10. He lives only for himself.   E ....
11. He lives a simple and austere existence.   A ....
12. He bootlicks the rich and powerful.   S ....
13. He is a false leader of the common people.   D ....
14. He's not sure whether or not God exists.   A ....
15. He claims that life is completely futile.   F ....
16. She's a masculine woman, big and muscular.   A ....
17. She has a sharp tongue and a vicious temper.   V ....
18. He has good taste in food.   G ....
19. He's extremely handsome.   A ....
20. He's coarse and uncouth.   V ....
21. He's a beginner in his profession.   T ....
22. He's a student of words.   PH ....
23. He says he can see things that you can't.   C ....
24. He's an authoritative judge and critic in some fine art or other area of excellence.   C ....
25. He collects stamps.   PH ....

ANSWERS: (1) atheist; (2) virtuoso; (3) numismatist; (4) esthete; (5) pedant; (6) judas; (7) coquette; (8) circe; (9) martinet; (10) egoist; (11) ascetic; (12) sycophant; (13) demagogue; (14) agnostic; (15) futilitarian; (16) amazon; (17) virago; (18) gourmet; (19) adonis; (20) vulgarian; (21) tyro; (22) philologist; (23) clairvoyant; (24) connoisseur; (25) philatelist

IX
Reinforce Your Knowledge

Ready for another try at the same words? Check the one adjective out of three offered that most nearly fits each noun.

1. *coquette*   sincere, flirtatious, talkative
2. *circe*   untrustworthy, unapproachable, nagging
3. *amazon*   feminine, alluring, big
4. *virago*   fierce, docile, feminine
5. *adonis*   feminine, good-looking, wasteful
6. *judas*   untrustworthy, unapproachable, unassuming
7. *futilitarian*   optimistic, pessimistic, indifferent
8. *vulgarian*   courteous, crude, clever
9. *pedant*   corrective, sentimental, soft-hearted
11. *egoist*   ambitious, boring, self-centered
11. *ascetic*   puny, puerile, puritanical
12. *esthete*   talkative, tasteful, triumphant
13. *demagogue*   traitorous, troublemaking, temperate
14. *martinet*   reckless, easygoing, demanding
15. *sycophant*   sincere, hypocritical, handsome
16. *atheist*   irreligious, youthful, flattering
17. *agnostic*   god-fearing, skeptical, ambitious
18. *tyro*   expert, uncouth, unskillful
19. *virtuoso*   skilled, indifferent, alluring
20. *philologist*   selfish, ill-mannered, scholarly
21. *clairvoyant*   prophetic, protesting, fearful
22. *philatelist*   stamp-involved, coin-involved, book-involved
23. *numismatist*   stamp-involved, coin-involved, book-involved
24. *gourmet*   fastidious, vulgar, piggish
25. *connoisseur*   discriminating, ignorant, ambitious

ANSWERS: (1) flirtatious;   (2) untrustworthy;   (3) big;   (4) fierce;   (5) good-looking;   (6) untrustworthy; (7) pessimistic; (8) crude; (9) corrective; (10) self-centered; (11) puritanical; (12) tasteful; (13) troublemaking; (14) demanding; (15) hypocritical; (16) irreligious; (17) skeptical; (18) unskillful; (19) skilled; (20) scholarly; (21) prophetic; (22) stamp-involved; (23) coin-involved; (24) fastidious; (25) discriminating

X
Further Reinforcement

Every time you test your learning and correct your errors or misconceptions you nail down a little more securely your familiarity with these colorful words. In this final test, therefore, you should be so nearly expert that you can make a perfect, or nearly perfect, score. Can you meet the challenge?

Choose the letter of the area from Column II that each person in Column I is involved in.

I	II
1. *coquette*	a. strength
2. *circe*	b. uselessness
3. *amazon*	c. obedience
4. *virago*	d. austere existence
5. *adonis*	e. preciseness
6. *judas*	f. skepticism
7. *futilitarian*	g. gaining experience
8. *vulgarian*	h. all beauty
9. *pedant*	i. stamps
10. *egoist*	j. language
11. *ascetic*	k. destruction of males
12. *esthete*	l. insincere flattery
13. *demagogue*	m. political power
14. *martinet*	n. marriage
15. *sycophant*	o. flirting

16. *atheist*	p. coarseness
17. *agnostic*	q. top performance
18. *tyro*	r. self-interest
19. *virtuoso*	s. extrasensory perception
20. *philologist*	t. food
21. *clairvoyant*	u. betrayal
22. *philatelist*	v. high quality
23. *numismatist*	w. male beauty
24. *gourmet*	x. coins
25. *connoisseur*	y. godlessness
	z. nagging

ANSWERS: (1) o; (2) k; (3) a; (4) z; (5) w;
(6) u; (7) b; (8) p; (9) e; (10) r;
(11) d; (12) h; (13) m; (14) c; (15)
l; (16) y; (17) f; (18) g; (19) q;
(20) j; (21) s; (22) i; (23) x; (24) t;
(25) v

We have discussed with you, and thoroughly tested you on, twenty-five intensely human words about human characteristics, professions, avocations, philosophies, and attitudes. These words are dynamic, meaningful, warm to the touch, pulsating with life. They describe your friends and enemies, your acquaintances and colleagues—perhaps yourself on occasion?

These words are valuable. Watch for them in your reading; listen for them in conversation. Use them yourself in your speech and writing—you will be delighted to discover how compactly and forcefully they express precisely what you want to say.

Words for Phobias and Manias

We touched on a number of normal human characteristics in the last chapter. Now we turn to a few of the abnormalities of the human mind, to the words that particularize mental peculiarities, neuroses, phobias, and mild or violent personality disorders.

I

Let us discuss, first, five of the most common manias: *kleptomania, pyromania, dipsomania, megalomania,* and *monomania.*

1. The *pyromaniac* (py′-rō-MAY′-nee-ak) has a strange and morbid passion for fire. He will burn down a house with no slightest sense of malice, but merely because he is fascinated by the flames.

2. The *dipsomaniac* (dip′-sō-MAY′-nee-ak) has an uncontrollable compulsion to drink. His vice is a good deal

more than a socially pleasant habit, of course. It is an emotional problem, and he must drink and get drunk whether he really wants to or not.

3. The *megalomaniac* (meg-ə-lō-MAY'-nee-ak) has a conviction that he is Napoleon or Caesar, that he has enormous wealth, or even, sometimes, that he is God. He is continually obsessed by delusions of grandeur.

4. The *monomaniac* (mon'-ō-MAY'-nee-ak) is unbalanced in just one area; on everything else except his own pet and particular delusion he may be completely normal.

5. The *kleptomaniac* (klep'-tō-MAY'-nee-ak) has a compulsion to steal. The victim of this aberration may be wealthy, and the object stolen may be worthless; moreover, the kleptomaniac never has any use for the lifted trinkets, nor any plans for their disposal. He just can't help taking them.

II

Write in the blank lines the "maniac" described by each of the following sentences:

1. He can't take one drink and then stop.   ....
2. He is mentally deranged on one subject.   ....
3. She is apt to steal any little object that she sees.   ....
4. He imagines he is God.   ....
5. It is dangerous to leave him alone with matches.   ....

ANSWERS: (1) dipsomaniac;   (2) monomaniac;   (3) kleptomaniac;   (4) megalomaniac;   (5) pyromaniac

III

What's your pet phobia? You haven't any? Don't be too sure. How about your startled-turtle habit of ducking under the bedclothes when the lightning crackles? Or your shudders when a snake crosses your path? Or possibly you edge away from the tops of tall buildings because height makes you feel funny?

If you are an average man you have, not one, but 2.21 phobias.

If you are an average woman you have 3.55 phobias.

Here is a list of the twelve most common phobias. You need not try to remember them, as they will hardly ever be useful to you unless you are a psychiatrist, in which case you already know them.

ceraunophobia	morbid dread of thunder
astraphobia	morbid dread of lightning
ophidiophobia	morbid dread of snakes
nyctophobia	morbid dread of darkness
acrophobia	morbid dread of heights
pyrophobia	morbid dread of fire
aquaphobia	morbid dread of water
ailurophobia	morbid dread of cats
cynophobia	morbid dread of dogs
agoraphobia	morbid dread of open spaces
triskaidekaphobia	morbid dread of the number thirteen
claustrophobia	morbid dread of close spaces

Three of these phobias are particularly common:

1. *Claustrophobia* (klawss′-trə-FŌ-bee-ə). The victim feels choked by small rooms or crowded or confined places. If there is not plenty of open space around him, his discomfort is acute; he may even go into a panic.

2. *Agoraphobia* (ag′-ə-rə-FŌ′-bee-ə). Contrarily, someone suffering from this problem cannot stand open spaces—very large rooms, public areas that have few people (empty theaters, for example), etc. He finds it painful, if not impossible, to walk across a deserted ball field. He is terrified, in short, by limitless horizons.

3. *Acrophobia* (ak′-rə-FŌ′-bee-ə). The person burdened with this fear is panic-stricken by heights. He cannot mount higher than the third or fourth step of a ladder, cannot look out of the top windows of a tall building, is

terrified of rapidly ascending elevators, would rather die
than take a plane trip.

IV

Four more people with emotional or mental problems:

1. The *hypochondriac* (hy'-pō-KON'-dree-ak) contin-
ully complains about imaginary ills. A heart flutter means
heart failure. A headache is a brain tumor. An upset
stomach indicates gastric ulcers or cancer. The only real
problem is, of course, a morbid imagination.

The ailment: *hypochondria* (hy'-pō-KON'-dree-ə)

2. The *amnesiac* (am-NEE'-zee-ak) suffers from loss of
memory. The cause is often a blow on the head or some
sudden emotional shock, after which the victim's past becomes a complete blank. He cannot even recognize his
family and closest friends. In time, with treatment, there
is usually a recovery.

The ailment: *amnesia* (am-NEE'-zhə)

3. The *somnambulist* (səm-NAM'-byə-list) walks in
his sleep.

The ailment: *somnambulism* (səm-NAM'-byə-liz-
əm)

4. The *insomniac* (in-SOM'-nee-ak) is habitually af-
flicted with wakefulness at times when he wishes to sleep.

The ailment: *insomnia* (in-SOM'-nee-ə)

V

Who would be most likely to say the following?

1. "What a night. I didn't sleep a wink!"   ....

2. "I walked around the room last night?
   Why, I was fast asleep."   ....

3. "Who am I? I've completely forgotten
   my name."   ....

4. "I don't care what the doctor says. I
   know I've got heart trouble."   ....

5. "I can't live in an apartment on the fifth floor. Isn't there anything vacant lower down?" ....

6. "I'm getting out of here. This place is so small I think the walls are going to crush me!" ....

7. "No thanks, I can't go fishing with you on that enormous lake. It goes on forever!" ....

ANSWERS: (1) insomniac; (2) somnambulist; (3) amnesiac; (4) hypochondriac; (5) acrophobe; (6) claustrophobe; (7) agoraphobe

VI

Four victims of very serious mental illness:

1. The *manic-depressive* (man'-ək-də-PRESS'-iv) has alternating moods of black depression and wild, uncontrollable exaltation or excitability. Changes are unpredictable and come without warning.

The illness: *manic-depression* (man'-ək-də-PRESH'-ən)

2. The *schizophrenic* (skiz'-ə-FREN'-ək) is a split or divided personality. He loses contact with his environment, lives in an unreal world of his own making, and often imagines he is someone else.

The illness: *schizophrenia* (skiz'-ə-FREEN'-yə)

3. The *melancholiac* (mel'-ən-KŌ'-lee-ak) has fallen into a fixed condition of despondency. He often thinks of, or attempts, suicide.

The illness: *melancholia* (mel'-ən-KŌ'-lee-ə)

4. The *paranoiac* (pair'-ə-NOY'-ak) has delusions of persecution. He imagines that people are trying to poison him, that he is being pursued by enemies, that everyone is against him.

The illness: *paranoia* (pair'-ə-NOY'-ə)

VII

According to Freudian psychology, the person who has grown up without successfully adjusting to the parent-child relationship or to his own place in the family constellation may develop either of the following:

1. An *Oedipus* (ED′-ə-pəs) *complex*. The male so burdened is the typical "mama's boy" who has been overprotected and overbabied and prevented from maturing emotionally. Unconsciously, according to the Freudians, he has a repressed desire to kill his father and marry his mother.

2. An *Electra* (ə-LEK′-trə) *complex*. This is the female version of the Oedipal problem—the girl is hostile to her mother, in love with her father.

VIII

Can you match the problem area with the name of the disturbance?

DISTURBANCE	PROBLEM AREA
1. *pyromania*	a. grandeur
2. *dipsomania*	b. illness
3. *megalomania*	c. sleepwalking
4. *monomania*	d. one single obsession
5. *kleptomania*	e. hilarity followed by gloom
6. *hypochondria*	f. fire
7. *amnesia*	g. no contact with reality
8. *somnambulism*	h. persecution
9. *insomniac*	i. attachment to mother
10. *manic-depression*	j. thievery
11. *schizophrenia*	k. open areas
12. *melancholia*	l. high places
13. *paranoia*	m. confined areas
14. *Oedipus complex*	n. memory
15. *Electra complex*	o. liquor
16. *claustrophobia*	p. attachment to father

17. *agoraphobia*   q. overwhelming sadness
18. *acrophobia*   r. sleeplessness

ANSWERS: (1) f;   (2) o;   (3) a;   (4) d;   (5) j;
          (6) b;   (7) n;   (8) c;   (9) r;   (10) e;
          (11) g;   (12) q;   (13) h;   (14) i;   (15)
          p;   (16) m;   (17) k;   (18) l

IX

Write the word that fits each definition. Initial letters
are offered to prod your memory.

1. M ....   Continued gloom and depression
2. M ....   Moods of violent excitement alter-
                       nating with black depression
3. A ....   Loss of memory
4. S ....   Walking and performing other ac-
                       tions during sleep
5. D ....   Uncontrollable craving for alcoholic
                       liquor
6. H ....   Morbid anxiety about one's health
7. P ....   Delusions of persecution
8. E ....   Early and abnormal attachment of a
                       girl for her father, with hostility to
                       her mother
9. K ....   Uncontrollable propensity to steal
                       articles of little value
10. M .... Delusions of grandeur
11. I .... Chronic inability to fall asleep
12. M .... Obsession in a single area
13. P .... Uncontrollable need to set fires
14. S .... Mental derangement characterized
                       by loss of contact with reality; split
                       personality
15. C .... Morbid dread of confined places
16. A .... Morbid dread of open spaces
17. O .... Unresolved attachment to mother
                       with accompanying hatred of father
18. A .... Morbid dread of heights

ANSWERS: (1)   melancholia;   (2)   manic-depression;
(3) amnesia;   (4) somnambulism;   (5) dipsomania;   (6) hypochondria;   (7) paranoia;
(8) Electra   complex;   (9)   kleptomania;
(10) megalomania;   (11) insomnia;   (12)
monomania;   (13) pyromania;   (14) schizophrenia;   (15) claustrophobia;   (16) agoraphobia;   (17) Oedipus complex;   (18) acrophobia

After such a chapter as this, you may think that we are
advocating the use of long and difficult words. But the
words we have discussed here are the only ones that accurately describe the troubles and disorders that afflict
many people. There are no substitutes for most of them.

But let this rule generally hold. Never, or at least almost never, use a long word where a short one will do.
Words, as you well know, are to express your thoughts,
not to conceal them. The greatest poems and the greatest
speeches, whether it is Robert Burns's "My love is like a
red, red rose" or Patrick Henry's "Give me liberty or give
me death" all have the power and charm of simplicity.
Try to avoid the too frequent use of such Latin words as
juxtaposition, animadvert, salutation, recapitulate. They
tend to make your style heavy, dry, and pedantic. Short
Anglo-Saxon words have force—*gift* instead of *donation;
poor* instead of *impecunious.* There is a simple beauty in
ship, shop, walk, free, earth, mate, man, friend. The Latin
and Greek words are important to know, but should be
used with discretion, and never to overwhelm a reader or
listener.

Simplicity and directness in language are always effective.

Words About Your Feelings

During the last few chapters we have been dealing with all kinds of people—with their peculiarities, their mental quirks, their philosophies, their ideas. Now let us deal with ideas alone. Or shall we get more personal, and consider the terms that describe *your* thoughts, *your* feelings, *your* attitudes and emotions?

Consider these five words:
nostalgia (nos-TAL'-jə)
satiated (SAY'-shee-ay'-təd)
benevolence (bə-NEV'-ə-lənce)
frustration (frus-TRAY'-shən)
lethargy (LETH'-ər-jee)

I

Are any of these strange to you? Consider them in sentences that give a hint to their meanings:

1. He was overcome with a wave of *nostalgia* whenever he thought of his boyhood years in Scotland.
2. The huge dinner left him *satiated*.
3. That morning he was at peace with the world; his attitude toward all mankind was one of *benevolence*.
4. All life, he claims, is *frustration*. The gods seem bent on mischievously thwarting his hopes and plans.
5. His illness left him in a state of *lethargy;* all ambition, interest, desire were gone.

II

Take the italicized words in Section I and write each one next to its definition.

1. .... State of apathy or indifference
2. .... Severe homesickness; a longing for the pleasant past
3. .... Desire for the welfare of others; charitableness
4. .... Filled beyond natural desire; glutted
5. .... Failure or inability to attain something desired

ANSWERS: (1) lethargy;   (2) nostalgia;   (3) benevolence;   (4) satiated;   (5) frustration

III

Five more words will now be treated in the same way. Again, try to figure out their meanings from the context of the sentences in which they appear.

enervated (EN'-ər-vay'-təd)
weltschmerz (VELT'-shmairtz)
ennui (AHN'-wee)
compunction (kəm-PUNK'-shən)
antipathy (an-TIP'-ə-thee)

1. His all-night vigil completely *enervated* him.
2. Adolescents are often rather pessimistic about the future of humanity. This *weltschmerz* is a natural result of their maturing minds and bodies.
3. Never had her life been so stagnant and empty. Never had she been so filled with *ennui*.
4. He had no *compunctions* about cheating his fellow-man.
5. He had a violent *antipathy* to all political theories smacking, however faintly, of communism.

IV

Can you pair off each of our new words with its definition below?

1. .... Literally, world pain; sadness from a gloomy world philosophy
2. .... An instinctive feeling of aversion or dislike
3. .... Self-reproach for wrongdoing; slight regret
4. .... Deprived of physical, nervous, and emotional energy
5. .... A feeling of listless weariness resulting from satiety, boredom, or inactivity

ANSWERS: (1) weltschmerz; (2) antipathy; (3) compunction; (4) enervated; (5) ennui

V

Here is a third group for study in the same way.
supercilious (soo'-pər-SIL'-ee-əs)
vindictive (vin-DIK'-tiv)
misogynist (mə-SAHJ'-ə-nist)
misanthrope (MISS'-ən-thrōp)
vicariously (vy-KAIR'-ee-əs-lee)

1. You are too *supercilious;* what makes you think you're so superior?

2. Be careful not to hurt her feelings, for she'll never forgive you. You know how *vindictive* some women are.

3. Queer chap—I think he's a *misogynist.* That's probably why he's never had a girl friend.

4. At heart, he's a *misanthrope.* No wonder he has no friends.

5. Since his accident he has been unable to take part in the sports that he used to love. Now he reads the sports page and enjoys tennis, golf, and baseball *vicariously.*

VI

Again, match each word to its definition.

1. .... Manner of experiencing something indirectly instead of directly
2. .... A hater of mankind
3. .... A hater of women
4. .... Disposed to revenge; retaliatory
5. .... Lofty with pride; haughtily contemptuous

ANSWERS: (1) vicariously;   (2) misanthrope;   (3) misogynist;   (4) vindictive;   (5) supercilious

VII

Now let's try a reinforcing exercise with all fifteen words. Check your response to each question.

1. When you have a feeling of *lethargy,* are you full of bounce, pep, and ambition?   Yes...... No......

2. Is *nostalgia* a yearning for the past?   Yes...... No......

3. Do kindly people often feel *benev-olent?*   Yes...... No......

4. When you haven't eaten for a long time, do you feel *satiated?*   Yes...... No......

5. Is *frustration* an unpleasant feeling?   Yes...... No......

6. Do pessimistic people often experience *weltschmerz?*   Yes...... No......

7. Do you feel *antipathy* to people you like?   Yes...... No......

8. Does a cruel and insensitive person have any *compunction* about mistreating others?   Yes...... No......

9. Is it normal to wake up *enervated* after a good night's sleep?   Yes...... No......

10. If nothing seems exciting or worthwhile is it justifiable to experience *ennui?*   Yes...... No......

11. Is living *vicariously* less fulfilling than direct experience?   Yes...... No......

12. Does a *misanthrope* hate everyone?   Yes...... No......

13. Does a *misogynist* enjoy the company of females?   Yes...... No......

14. Does a *vindictive* person forgive easily?   Yes...... No......

15. Does a *supercilious* person usually feel superior to others?   Yes...... No......

ANSWERS: (1) No; (2) Yes; (3) Yes; (4) No; (5) Yes; (6) Yes; (7) No; (8) No; (9) No; (10) Yes; (11) Yes; (12) Yes; (13) No; (14) No; (15) Yes

VIII

Ready for more reinforcement? Write S if a pair of words are essentially the *same* in meaning, O if they are more or less *opposed*.

1. *lethargy*	....	energy
2. *nostalgia*	....	homesickness
3. *benevolence*	....	ill will
4. *satiated*	....	full
5. *frustration*	....	satisfaction
6. *weltschmerz*	....	happiness
7. *antipathy*	....	affection
8. *compunctions*	....	scruples
9. *enervated*	....	tired
10. *ennui*	....	boredom
11. *vicariously*	....	actually
12. *misanthrope*	....	philanthropist
13. *misogynist*	....	Don Juan
14. *vindictive*	....	forgiving
15. *supercilious*	....	humble

ANSWERS: (1) o;   (2) s;   (3) o;   (4) s;   (5) o;
          (6) o;   (7) o;   (8) s;   (9) s;   (10) s;
          (11) o;   (12) o;   (13) o;   (14) o;   (15) o

IX

A very useful exercise, one that helps you use words in a variety of ways, requires you to experiment with different parts of speech—noun, adjective, adverb, verb. Can you make the proper changes asked for below? An illustrative phrase or sentence and, where possible, an analogy are offered to help you.

1. Change *lethargy* to an adjective to fit into the following phrase: A .... attitude.
   (*neuralgia—neuralgic*)
2. *Nostalgia* to an adjective: A .... feeling.
   (*claustrophobia—claustrophobic*)
3. *Benevolence* to an adverb: He beamed ....
   (*impotence—impotently*)
4. *Satiated* to a negative adjective ending in -*ble:* He is an .... reader.
   (*estimated—inestimable*)

5. *Satiated* to a noun ending in *-ty:* I've had a .... of motion pictures.
(*anxious—anxiety*)

6. *Frustration* to a verb: Why do you try to .... me?
(*appreciation—appreciate*)

7. *Antipathy* to an adjective: I am .... to such ideas.
(*sympathy—sympathetic*)

8. *Enervated* to a noun: The cause of his ....
(*saturated—saturation*)

9. *Vicariously* to an adjective: A .... thrill.
(*famously—famous*)

10. *Misanthrope* to another noun denoting the person: He is a ....
(ends in *-ist*)

11. *Misanthrope* to a noun denoting the philosophy: What is the cause of his ....?
(*philanthropist—philanthropy*)

12. *Misogynist* to a noun denoting the philosophy: What is the cause of his ....?
(*botanist—botany*)

13. *Vindictive* to a noun: I dislike him mainly for his
....
(*active—activeness*)

14. *Supercilious* to a noun: Your .... will make you lose many friends.
(*fastidious—fastidiousness*)

ANSWERS: (1) lethargic (lə-THAHR′-jik); (2) nostalgic (nə-STAL′-jik; (3) benevolently (bə-NEV′-ə-lənt-lee); (4) insatiable (in-SAY′-shee-ə-bəl); (5) satiety (sə-TY′-ə-tee); (6) frustrate (FRUSS′-trate); (7) antipathetic (an′-tee-pə-THET′-ik); (8) enervation (ən′-ər-VAY′-shən); (9) vicarious (vy-KAIR′-ee-əs); (10) misanthropist (mə-SAN′-thrə-pist);

(11) misanthropy (mə-SAN'-thrə-pee); (12) misogyny (mə-SAHJ'-ə-nee); (13) vindictiveness (vin-DIK'-tiv-nəss); (14) superciliousness (soo'-pər-SIL'-ee-əs-nəss)

X

Now let's sock it home. If all your work with, and exposure to, the words in this chapter have finally made you master of them, you will be able, without doubt or hesitation, to match the *statement of feeling* to each noun below.

NOUNS	STATEMENT OF FEELING
1. *lethargy*	a. "I can't do it!"
2. *nostalgia*	b. "You do it, I'll watch."
3. *benevolence*	c. "All is boredom."
4. *satiety*	d. "I hate everyone!"
5. *frustration*	e. "I'm exhausted, worn out."
6. *weltschmerz*	f. "I hate women!"
7. *antipathy*	g. "I wish I were home."
8. *compunction*	h. "I can't stand it!"
9. *ennui*	i. "I'll get even!"
10. *enervation*	j. "I can't move, can't respond."
11. *vicariousness*	k. "You're dirt!"
12. *misanthropy*	l. "The world is a sad place."
13. *misogyny*	m. "No more, please."
14. *vindictiveness*	n. "I'd better not."
15. *superciliousness*	o. "I wish the best for you."

ANSWERS: (1) j; (2) g; (3) o; (4) m; (5) a; (6) l; (7) h; (8) n; (9) c; (10) e; (11) b; (12) d; (13) f; (14) i; (15) k

Compactly, richly, effectively—and as no others can— these words express deep, living, glowing ideas. Without them you might have to fumble to express what you mean.

Once you know the *exact* word, your ideas come across in simple and immediately understandable clarity.

With a well-stocked arsenal of words at your command, you can become a more powerful, more influential thinker, writer, and speaker.

X	X	X	X	X	X	X
X	X	X	X	X	X	14
15	16	17	18	19	20	21
22	23	24	25	26	27	28
29	30					

Words That End in "Ology"

Traveling at the rate of 186,000 miles a second, a ray of light started toward the earth with the message that a star had exploded somewhere in space. Thirteen centuries passed by before it arrived. Goethe, Shakespeare, Galileo, and King Arthur's Court all came and went. Napoleon strode over Europe like a colossus, lost his kingdom and died. America was discovered. Great wars began and ceased and began again, while this glimmer of light was racing on to tell our astronomers of a world-shaking catastrophe that had happened in the constellation of Hercules.

This message was read and understood. And that is the triumph of the mind of man.

His intellect can weigh the sun and measure the heat from the farthest star. His eyes can see a billion miles into space and they can also explore the infinitesimal world of electrons. Man has struggled for his knowledge of medicine and archaeology and geology and the multitude of sciences. We, by the miracle of words, can open some of these doors, and if they are so much as barely open, we may be tempted to walk in.

I
The Fields of Human Knowledge

1. *Anthropology* (an'-thrō-POL'-ǝ-jee). This word we have had before and you will recognize it as "the science of mankind" in general, his habits, history, distribution, culture.

2. *Geology* (jee-OL'-ǝ-jee). The meaning of this word is crystal clear when we know that the "geo" comes from the Greek *geos,* "earth," plus *logos,* "study" or "science." *Geology,* then, is the science of the structure, forces, and history of that whirling planet we call earth.

3. *Archaeology* (ahr'-kee-OL'-ǝ-jee). This is the science of antiquities. It deals with the old records that man leaves in such forms as buildings and pottery and in the physical remains of his industries. The key to the language of the Aztecs of ancient Mexico, for example, has not been fully discovered, but *archaeologists* can learn much of the story of these people from the ruins they left. (Greek *archaios,* "ancient," and therefore "the study of ancient things.")

4. *Embryology* (em'-bree-OL'-ǝ-jee). In the early stages of pre-natal development, the unborn child is called an *embryo.* Once more the Greeks have helped us, for *en* in their language means "in," and *bryein,* "swell"; so, literally, the word means "to swell inside," which is just what happens in pregnancy. An *embryologist,* then, deals with the beginnings of life.

5. *Entomology* (en'-tǝ-MOL'-ǝ-jee). When you know that *entomon* is Greek for "insect," the rest is easy to guess. The *entomologists* have given us a wealth of knowledge about the home life, sex habits, and social customs of bees, ants, butterflies, and other members of the species.

6. *Ethnology* (eth-NOL′-ə-jee).   White men, brown men, black men, yellow men. What is their history? Where did they come from? Where do they live? How do they differ in mind, culture, characteristics? These are problems for the *ethnologist* to solve. From Greek, *ethnos,* "race."

7. *Etymology* (et′-ə-MOL′-ə-jee). You will recall that this is the study of the history and origin of words.

8. *Ornithology* (awr′-nə-THOL′-ə-jee). If you are told that *ornis* is Greek for "bird," you can find your own meaning. The lives and habits of eagles and whippoorwills, tanagers and sparrows, hawks and seagulls—all such are the province of the *ornithologist.*

9. *Philology* (fə-LOL′-ə-jee). This word we are already familiar with. The *philologist* covers the entire field of words and language, the whole area of linguistics.

10. *Psychology* (sy-KOL′-ə-jee). Once more let's leaf over the pages of our Greek lexicon, and we find *psyche,* "soul," "mind." So the *psychologist* is a student of, and an authority on, the human mind, and human behavior in all of its aspects.

II
Review Your Learning

Here are the ten fields of human knowledge once again, in simple chart form, with the scientist in parentheses next to each one. Can you review in your mind the area of interest of each scientist in preparation for a reinforcing test?

THE FIELD	THE AREA
1. *anthropology* (*anthropologist*)	....
2. *geology* (*geologist*)	....
3. *archaeology* (*archaeologist*)	....
4. *embryology* (*embryologist*)	....
5. *entomology* (*entomologist*)	....
6. *ethnology* (*ethnologist*)	....
7. *etymology* (*etymologist*)	....

8. *ornithology* (*ornithologist*) ....
9. *philology* (*philologist*) ....
10. *psychology* (*psychologist*) ....

III
Where Does One Turn?

If you wished the answer to each of the following questions, to which of the specialists in Section II would you turn for your information?

1. What does the unborn baby look like during the third week of its development? ....

2. How many Mayan ruins are there in Central America? ....

3. What makes human beings behave the way they do? ....

4. What kind of rock is found in Tennessee? ....

5. Is it true that the owl is wiser than other birds? ....

6. What did the men of the Stone Age look like? ....

7. What is the life span of an ant? ....

8. What is the derivation or origin of the word *boycott*? ....

9. How many different languages are spoken in Europe? ....

10. Where are the yellow races found in greatest abundance? ....

ANSWERS: (1) embryologist; (2) archaeologist; (3) psychologist; (4) geologist; (5) ornithologist; (6) anthropologist; (7) entomologist; (8) etymologist; (9) philologist; (10) ethnologist

IV
Don't Stop Now!

There are still many things you can do with these words. Say them aloud, many times. That is the first step toward making them your own. If you aren't perfectly comfortable with their pronunciation, you won't dare to use them.

Try spelling them. Get a friend or a member of your family to help you by dictating the words while you write them. Each step is a clincher that helps hold the words more firmly in your mind, helps you feel more at home with them.

Experiment with the etymologies. Greek *geos* means "earth." How easy it is then to read the meaning of *geography, geopolitics, geometry.*

Anthropos is "mankind"; thus *misanthropy, philanthropy,* and *anthropoid* (similar to man) fall right in place.

Archaios, "ancient," gives us *archaic* (ancient, no longer used, old-fashioned), and *archetype* (the ancient, or original model), as well as *archaeology.*

Psyche, "soul" or "mind," produces words like *psychic, psychiatry, psychoanalysis, psychotic,* as well as *psychology.* Once you recognize the root, the word itself can no longer be a complete mystery to you.

The *philologist* loves words—from *philein,* "to love," and *logos,* one of whose meanings is "word" (the other is "study of"). *Philadelphia* is the City of Brotherly Love; a *philatelist* loves stamps; a *bibliophile* loves books; a *philanthropist* loves mankind; a *philosopher* loves wisdom; a *philtre* is a love potion. We repeat: Know the root, and the word is no longer a mystery.

So let's end the chapter by giving you a chance to fix the roots and meanings in your mind. Can you match the two columns below?

1. *anthropos (anthropology)*   a. earth
2. *archaios (archaeology)*   b. race
3. *geos (geology)*   c. insect
4. *bryein (embryology)*   d. bird

5. *entomon* (*entomology*)   e. mind, soul
6. *ethnos* (*ethnology*)   f. mankind
7. *ornis* (*ornithology*)   g. word, study of
8. *philein* (*philology*)   h. to love
9. *psyche* (*psychology*)   i. to swell
10. *logos* (*etymology*)   j. ancient

ANSWERS: (1) f; (2) j; (3) a; (4) i; (5) c; (6) b; (7) d; (8) h; (9) e; (10) g

X	X	X	X	X	X	X
X	X	X	X	X	X	X
15	16	17	18	19	20	21
22	23	24	25	26	27	28
29	30					

Words for Human Traits

Men and women have so many forms of behavior, and such a multitude of varied characteristics and points of view, that they have inspired a host of descriptive adjectives. We will introduce the new words first in a series of simple sentences to give at least a hint to their meanings.

I

1. The *loquacious* (lō-KWAY'-shəs) girl talks incessantly.
2. The *gullible* (GULL'-ə-bəl) housewife believes everything a canvasser tells her.
3. The *suave* (SWAHV) talker can persuade you that black is white.
4. The *pompous* (POM'-pəs) person seems overwhelmed with a sense of his own importance.
5. The *esthetic* (es-THET'-ik) artist has dedicated his life to beauty.

6. The *taciturn* (TAS′-ə-turn) husband answers his wife in grunts and monosyllables, if at all.

7. The *opinionated* (ə-PIN′-yə-nay′-təd) fool has a mind so finally made up that neither hell nor high water can make him change it.

8. The *phlegmatic* (fleg-MAT′-ik) person can't get excited over anything.

9. The *erudite* (AIR′-ə-dite) man is full of book learning.

10. The *complacent* (kəm-PLAY′-sənt) fellow is sure that everything is going to come out all right.

11. The *punctilious* (punk-TILL′-ee-əs) hostess worries if so much as one fork is out of place on her perfectly set table.

12. The *indefatigable* (in′-de-FAT′-ə-gə-bəl) worker seems capable of getting along on four hours' sleep a day.

13. The *vapid* (VAP′-id) talker's conversation is completely boring.

14. The *iconoclastic* (eye-kon′-ə-KLASS′-tik) critic carps at such institutions as government, marriage, and religion.

15. The *misanthropic* (miss′-ən-THROP′-ik) cynic hates the world and everybody in it.

16. The *puerile* (PYOO′-ər-əl) practical joker may have grown up physically, but is still a child emotionally.

17. The *ascetic* (a-SET′-ik) person lives in a hut and likes it.

II

These words have been used in sentences that aim at giving you enough of a clue to spark your interest in figuring out the possible meanings. How successfully can you find the italicized word in Section I that best fits each of the following definitions?

1. Completely self-satisfied; smug   ....
2. Smooth and pleasant in manner; bland; gracious; smoothly ingratiating   ....

3. By temperament, not easily perturbed; calm; emotionally sluggish or unresponsive ....

4. One who assails or mocks traditional or cherished beliefs ....

5. Simple; credulous; easily deceived ....

6. Marked by assumed self-importance; pretentious ....

7. Appreciating or loving the beautiful; artistic ....

8. Characteristic of childhood; juvenile; immature and silly or trivial ....

9. Very learned; scholarly ....

10. Practicing extreme abstinence; austere and rigorous in self-denial or self-discipline ....

11. Extremely talkative ....

12. Habitually silent or unwilling to engage in conversation ....

13. Unduly attached to one's own opinions; obstinate in holding on to beliefs ....

14. Not exhausted by labor or exercise; never tiring ....

15. Hating mankind ....

16. Very exact or scrupulous in the observance of forms of etiquette, ceremony, or behavior ....

17. Utterly lacking in sparkle, flavor, or interest; empty and flat ....

ANSWERS: (1) complacent; (2) suave; (3) phlegmatic; (4) iconoclastic; (5) gullible; (6) pompous; (7) esthetic; (8) puerile; (9) erudite; (10) ascetic; (11) loquacious; (12) taciturn; (13) opinionated; (14) indefatigable; (15) misanthropic; (16) punctilious; (17) vapid

III

Our theory throughout this book, as you have no doubt already observed, is that the best way to learn new words effectively is the way that everyone, from infancy on, learns them—namely, by gradual, step-by-step increasing of understanding. It is the repeated contact with a word in many different contexts that finally makes you so familiar and comfortable with it that you eventually feel it was always in your vocabulary. It is at this point that you begin using the word in your thinking, speaking, and writing—and you do so unself-consciously, without effort, and so unexpectedly that sometimes you even surprise yourself.

You have now had two exposures to the seventeen words that comprise this chapter—once in a sentence, once in matching them to their definitions. Here is your third exposure: a series of phrases, each of which should produce a flash of recognition in you that helps you react with one of the seventeen words. Do not look back as you do this exercise—the initial letter of the word is a sufficient prod to your power to recall. Several of the adjectives will be required more than once.

In this exercise you should begin to feel the first surges of power and self-confidence as you zip through, writing each word as it is called for.

 1. Emotionally sluggish   P ....
 2. Practicing self-denial   A ....
 3. Disinclined to conversation   T ....
 4. Having an antipathy for mankind   M ....
 5. Easily duped   G ....
 6. Insipid   V ....
 7. Scholarly   E ....
 8. Talkative   L ....
 9. Precise in the observance of forms P ....
10. Ostentatiously self-important   P ....
11. Inane   V ....
12. Responsive to beauty   E ....

13. Descriptive of the attitude of one
    who attacks cherished beliefs as
    shams   I ....
14. Childish   P ....
15. Polished in manner   S ....
16. Stubbornly set in opinions   O ....
17. Self-satisfied   C ....
18. Attacking established traditions   I ....
19. Having an aversion for the human   M ....
    race
20. Tireless   I ....
21. Urbanely smooth and ingratiating   S ....
22. Contented with oneself and with
    things as they are   C ....

ANSWERS: (1) phlegmatic; (2) ascetic; (3) taciturn;
         (4) misanthropic; (5) gullible; (6) vapid;
         (7) erudite; (8) loquacious; (9) punctili-
         ous; (10) pompous; (11) vapid; (12)
         esthetic; (13) iconoclastic; (14) puerile;
         (15) suave; (16) opinionated; (17) com-
         placent; (18) iconoclasm; (19) misan-
         thropic; (20) indefatigable; (21) suave;
         (22) complacent

IV

Now test your increasing understanding of these seventeen words by marking each of the following statements
"true" or "false":

1. Talkative women are called *lo-
   quacious*.   True...... False......
2. Country yokels are as a rule
   suave.   True...... False......
3. The stereotype of the truckdriv-
   er is usually *esthetic*.   True...... False......
4. Enthusiastic people are usually
   taciturn.   True...... False......

5. The more impartial a man is, the more *opinionated* he sounds. True...... False......

6. *Phlegmatic* people usually become panicky in an emergency. True...... False......

7. *Pomposity* is usually amusing. True...... False......

8. College professors are often *erudite*. True...... False......

9. Smug people are never *complacent*. True...... False......

10. *Punctilious* people are sticklers for form. True...... False......

11. The beaver is an *indefatigable* worker. True...... False......

12. The conversation of a conceited bore is usually *vapid*. True...... False......

13. The attitude of young people is usually *iconoclastic*. True...... False......

14. *Misanthropic* remarks show a feeling of love and trust for people. True...... False......

15. *Puerile* behavior indicates maturity. True...... False......

16. An *ascetic* existence is given over to sensuality. True...... False......

17. A young child is apt to be *gullible*. True...... False......

ANSWERS: (1) true; (2) false; (3) false; (4) false; (5) false; (6) false; (7) true; (8) true; (9) false; (10) true; (11) true; (12) true; (13) true; (14) false; (15) false; (16) false; (17) true

V

Continuing your gradual reinforcement of understanding through stimulus and response, try a different type of test. Check the word or phrase that best completes each sentence.

1. *Loquacity* is an inordinate amount of:
   a. singing
   b. attention to details
   c. talking
2. *Gullible* people fall easy prey to:
   a. doctors
   b. used-car salesmen
   c. teachers
3. *Suave* men are experts at:
   a. home repair
   b. surfing
   c. getting along with women
4. *Pomposity* probably comes from:
   a. fear
   b. obesity
   c. vanity
5. Most likely to be *esthetic* is an:
   a. electrician
   b. aviator
   c. artist
6. *Taciturnity* would likely be found in:
   a. salesmen
   b. public speakers
   c. hermits
7. *Opinionated* assertions may likely lead to:
   a. marriage
   b. arguments
   c. truth
8. A *phlegmatic* person:
   a. sheds tears at an emotional play
   b. becomes hysterical in a crisis
   c. does not become easily emotional
9. *Erudite* men are most interested in:
   a. scholarly books
   b. light fiction
   c. the comics

10. People who are *complacent* about their jobs will:
    a. take it easy
    b. worry about their future
    c. keep an eye on the help-wanted ads

11. A *punctilious* person is a stickler for:
    a. originality
    b. courage
    c. proper etiquette

12. To be *indefatigable,* one usually needs a great amount of:
    a. money
    b. energy
    c. education

13. *Vapid* people are:
    a. boring
    b. successful
    c. quarrelsome

14. *Iconoclasts* are opposed to:
    a. change
    b. tradition
    c. reform

15. A *misanthrope* dislikes:
    a. people
    b. good food
    c. literature

16. Men are most likely to be *puerile* when:
    a. they don't get their own way
    b. they are reading
    c. they are eating

17. Most *ascetics* prefer to:
    a. drink excessively
    b. eat sparingly
    c. participate in orgies

ANSWERS: (1) c; (2) b; (3) c; (4) c; (5) c; (6) c; (7) b; (8) c; (9) a; (10) a; (11) c; (12) b; (13) a; (14) b; (15) a; (16) a; (17) b

VI

Ready for a final, and considerably harder, challenge?
Write the adjective we have studied that is essentially *opposed in meaning* to each of the following words or
phrases. Do you now feel sufficiently self-confident not to
look back at previous pages as you search your mind for
the answers?

1. taciturn ....
2. easily swayed to change one's
   mind ....
3. ignorant ....
4. philanthropic ....
5. blind to beauty ....
6. lazy ....
7. dissatisfied ....
8. conservative ....
9. mature ....
10. careless of etiquette; informal ....
11. voluptuous; pleasure-loving ....
12. boorish ....
13. modest, humble ....
14. loquacious ....
15. high-strung ....
16. skeptical ....
17. clever and interesting ....

ANSWERS: (1) loquacious; (2) opinionated; (3) erudite; (4) misanthropic; (5) esthetic; (6)
indefatigable; (7) complacent; (8) iconoclastic; (9) puerile; (10) punctilious;
(11) ascetic; (12) suave; (13) pompous;
(14) taciturn; (15) phlegmatic; (16) gullible; (17) vapid

VII

There are interesting etymologies behind many of the words in this chapter.

Suave: Latin *suavis,* "sweet" or "smooth."

Iconoclastic: Greek *eikon,* "idol"; *klaein,* "to break." An *iconoclast,* then, is a breaker of idols, or, in the modern sense, a breaker of traditions.

Pompous: Latin *pompa,* "parade" or "solemn procession."

Esthetic: Greek *aisthetikos,* "perceptive," became refined in our language until it referred to the finer feelings and perceptions in the field of art and culture.

Puerile: Latin *puer,* "boy." When a man is *puerile* he is acting like an ungrown boy.

Ascetic: Greek *asketikos,* "self-denying or self-disciplined for purposes of gymnastic excellence." Eventually, our English word took on a more general, all-inclusive meaning.

Loquacious: Latin *loquor,* "speak." *Eloquent* and *colloquial* come from the same root.

Taciturn: Latin *tacere,* "be silent."

Opinionated: Latin *opinio,* "thought" or "opinion." *Opinionated* came to mean too well provided with opinions, and, finally, stubborn or set in opinions.

Indefatigable: Latin *in,* "not," and *defatigare,* "to tire out."

Punctilious: Latin *punctum,* "point." *Punctilious* is used in our language to refer to someone who is very attentive to fine points. *Punctual* and *puncture* derive from the same root.

Vapid: Latin *vapidus,* "flavorless"—and *vapidus* itself is from Latin *vappa,* a wine that has lost its life or savor.

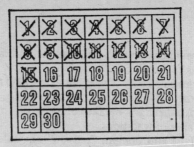

Words for Human Faults

Have you ever met the carefree young bachelor whose life seems to be one *peccadillo* after another? Does such a one have to be a man of some wealth, or can he follow his manner of life in the midst of *penury*? Do his successes with the opposite sex tend to give him a touch of *megalomania*? His life is certainly an interesting one: that is, if you consider that one *imbroglio* after another makes for interest. Just listen to him talk. His *braggadocio* may entertain his younger acquaintances, but it certainly becomes tiresome to his older friends.

I

Pronounce each word carefully:
1. *peccadillo* (pek'-ə-DIL'-ō)
2. *penury* (PEN'-yə-ree)
3. *megalomania* (meg'-ə-lə-MAY'-nee-ə)
4. *imbroglio* (im-BRŌ'-lyō)
5. *braggadocio* (brag'-ə-DŌ'-shee-ō)

II

From an analysis of the paragraph above can you match each word to its definition?
1. A complicated and embarrassing situation   ....
2. A slight sin   ....
3. Empty boasting   ....
4. Abject poverty   ....
5. Grandiose delusions of one's own importance   ....

ANSWERS: (1) imbroglio;   (2) peccadillo;   (3) braggadocio;   (4) penury;   (5) megalomania

III

What kind of person are you? Do you think money is a *panacea*? Do you feel your life has been a *fiasco*? What are some of your *idiosyncrasies*? Do you tend to *rationalize* rather than face the truth? Are there *anomalies* in your life that you would like to see removed? The answers to these questions may reveal a number of interesting things about your character.

IV

1. *panacea* (pan'-ə-SEE'-ə)
2. *fiasco* (fee-ASS'-kō)
3. *idiosyncrasy* (id'-ee-ə-SIN'-krə-see)
4. *rationalize* (RASH'-ə-nə-lize')
5. *anomaly* (ə-NOM'-ə-lee)

V

1. Something that is irregular or inconsistent   ....
2. A cure for all ills   ....

3. A miserable and ridiculous failure   ....
4. To react unconsciously with a worthy
   motive for a discreditable act   ....
5. A characteristic peculiarity   ....

ANSWERS: (1) anomaly;   (2) panacea;   (3) fiasco;
         (4) rationalize;   (5) idiosyncrasy

VI

Do you by chance have a neurotic friend who is so lazy
that he tends to *malinger?* Or one who belongs to the *élite*
and looks down his social nose at the *parvenus?* The conversation of such a person is apt to be *banal,* certainly not
as interesting as that of the *intelligentsia.* Or have you
ever been up against a politician who resorts to *jingoism*
and *chicanery* because he cannot gain his end by honest
means?

VII

1. *malinger* (mə-LING'-gər)
2. *élite* (ay'-LEET')
3. *parvenu* (PAR'-və-nōō)
4. *jingoism* (JING'-gō-iz-əm)
5. *intelligentsia* (in-tell'-ə-JEN'-see-ə)
6. *chicanery* (shə-KAY'-nə-ree)
7. *banal* (BAY'-nəl)

VIII

1. The best or most capable part of any
   group   ....
2. One who flaunts, somewhat vulgarly, new-
   ly attained wealth (used contemptuously)   ....
3. To feign sickness to shirk work or duty   ....

4. Favoring a warlike foreign policy ....
5. The intelligent and educated classes ....
6. Mean, petty trickery ....
7. Commonplace; without sparkle or originality ....

ANSWERS: (1) élite; (2) parvenu; (3) malinger; (4)
jingoism; (5) intelligentsia; (6) chicanery;
(7) banal

IX

You have had your first involvement with seventeen new words. Remember, your aim is to become more and more comfortable with new words by meeting them in different situations, working with them in different ways. So now let's try this: Review the preceding pages of this chapter, pronouncing the seventeen words aloud often enough to feel quite at home with them. Then, without further reference, write each one next to the phrase below that is closest in meaning to it. The initial letter is offered as a guide.

1. Extreme poverty or want P ....
2. The best É ....
3. A complete or humiliating failure F ....
4. Trickery C ....
5. To feign illness in order to escape
work M ....
6. To find a worthier motive for R ....
7. A deviation from type; an irregular-
ity A ....
8. Remedy for all diseases P ....
9. A bellicose foreign policy J ....
10. Educated and intellectual people I ....
11. Ordinary; dull B ....
12. Delusions of grandeur M ....
13. Pretentious boasting B ....
14. A slight or trifling sin P ....

15. A confused and complicated situation   I ....
16. A characteristic peculiarity   I ....
17. A *nouveau riche;* a newly wealthy person   P ....

ANSWERS: (1) penury; (2) élite; (3) fiasco; (4) chicanery; (5) malinger; (6) rationalize; (7) anomaly; (8) panacea; (9) jingoism; (10) intelligentsia; (11) banal; (12) megalomania; (13) braggadocio; (14) peccadillo; (15) imbroglio; (16) idiosyncrasy; (17) parvenu

X

Here's another exercise for still further reinforcement and continuing success. Check whether each pair below is nearly the *same* or *opposite* in meaning.

1. *peccadillo*	slight sin	Same......	Opposite......
2. *penury*	wealth	Same......	Opposite......
3. *megalomania*	humility	Same......	Opposite......
4. *imbroglio*	confusion	Same......	Opposite......
5. *braggadocio*	boasting	Same......	Opposite......
6. *panacea*	cure-all	Same......	Opposite......
7. *fiasco*	success	Same......	Opposite......
8. *idiosyncrasy*	peculiarity	Same......	Opposite......
9. *rationalize*	justify	Same......	Opposite......
10. *anomaly*	irregularity	Same......	Opposite......
11. *malinger*	pretend illness	Same......	Opposite......
12. *élite*	the worst	Same......	Opposite......
13. *parvenu*	*nouveau riche*	Same......	Opposite......
14. *jingoism*	pacifism	Same......	Opposite......
15. *intelligentsia*	the feeble-minded	Same......	Opposite......
16. *chicanery*	honesty	Same......	Opposite......
17. *banal*	original	Same......	Opposite......

ANSWERS: (1) same; (2) opposite; (3) opposite; (4) same; (5) same; (6) same; (7) opposite; (8) same; (9) same; (10) same; (11) same; (12) opposite; (13) same; (14) opposite; (15) opposite; (16) opposite; (17) opposite

XI

Note how other people have used some of these words:

1. As Professor Owen has remarked, there is no greater *anomaly* in nature than a bird that cannot fly.
   (DARWIN)

2. Owing to the disunion of the Fenians themselves, the rigor of the administration, and the treachery of informers, the (Irish) rebellion was a *fiasco*.
   (*The Encyclopedia Britannica*)

3. *Idiosyncrasies* are, however, frequent; thus we find that one person has an exceptional memory for sounds, another for colors, another for forms.
   (*The Encyclopedia Britannica*)

4. The chemists pretended it was the philosopher's stone, the physicians that it was an infallible *panacea*.
   (WHARTON)

5. The Koran attaches much importance to prayer—a fact which is somewhat *anomalous* in a system of religion so essentially fatalistic.
   (SPENCER)

6. Men who by legal *chicanery* cheat others out of their property.
   (SPENCER)

7. Who doesn't forgive? The virtuous Mrs. Grundy. She remembers her neighbors' *peccadilloes* to the third and fourth generations.
   (THACKERAY)

8. I have always observed through life that your *parvenu* it is who stickles for what he calls the genteel, and has the most squeamish abhorrence for what is frank and natural.
   (THACKERAY)

9. 'Tis low ebb with his accusers when such *peccadilloes* as these are put in to swell the charge.

(BISHOP OF ATTERBURY)

XII

You are now halfway through this book.

How is your work going? Do you feel you are making progress? Here are a few suggestions that may increase the speed of your achievement.

Try laying out a simple, definite but not overambitious plan for your daily study, if you haven't already done so. Choosing a fixed time each day for this work will be helpful. But if that should be impractical, then learn the fine art of using your spare moments. John Erskine, the famous author, trained himself to use all those minutes of the day that other people waste, and during these periods of salvaged time he wrote most of his novels.

Above all, make this present study a habit, like getting dressed or undressed, combing your hair or brushing your teeth, so that it will become a part of your life and you will turn to it as naturally as you have breakfast in the morning.

And here is a rule that busy men have found invaluable. Always plan your next day's work the night before.

✗	✗	✗	✗	✗	✗	✗
✗	✗	✗	✗	✗	✗	✗
✗	✗	17	18	19	20	21
22	23	24	25	26	27	28
29	30					

You Help to Create the American Language

We have now come to an interval, a halfway mark, in our consideration of words.

We can take a little time out to discuss the matter of who owns this language that we have been studying.

Well, you own it. And you. And you. The English language belongs to you. You made it. You are making it every day. You have invented upward of 600,000 usable English words, minus those that have been taken over from other languages. But even these were adopted by you. You have devised the queer spellings of English words. You have determined their pronunciations.

In English we are dealing with an inexact art, not an exact science. Even the mistakes of English are human. Some of our fantastic spellings in this book that you hold in your hand are due merely to the errors of ignorant type-setters who lived centuries ago. We have merely preserved and honored their misspellings. Pronunciations and meanings are frequently modified with just as little reason.

How then, specifically, do you control the language?

In this way: During this present year about five thousand new words will come into our language. Intense and dramatic times such as these are always prolific in breeding new words. The scholars won't mint or invent these new words. They will just pop up. The scholars will have nothing whatsoever to say about how they shall be pronounced or spelled, or what they shall mean. They will be pronounced and spelled and defined pretty much as the public pleases. If you were to ask the editor of the Funk & Wagnalls New Standard Dictionary or of Webster's or the Oxford or of any other, "Who decides about these new words?" this editor would answer, "You do," meaning, of course, the many millions of "you" who use our language.

Let's take a case in point. *Television* was invented and one of you thought up the word *telecast* as a parallel term to *broadcast*. Scholars called it a bastard type of word, half from the Greek *tele,* "far away," and half from the English word *cast,* but *telecast* it was just the same, thanks to the common people who included it in the current coin of their conversation.

In similar fashion—that is, by usage—old words completely change their meanings, nice words become coarse, and coarse words become respectable.

Slang, for instance, is a good example of the latter move on the part of words.

A great mass of our language was once the slang of the various gas house districts of the world. A large part of it came from over the railroad tracks. Purists and highbrows protested and fulminated against it, but little by little common usage made many of these words so respectable that the scholars were willing to use them and were forced to include them in the dictionaries.

Around 230 years ago, for example, Dean Swift was kicking (slang) at the then current use of such slang words as *bubble, sham, bully,* and *hips* as "a disgrace to our language." Now you and I use them very happily. Let us recite a few more that were once slang: *gin, boycott, cab, greenhorn, hoax, jingoist.*

You see, the masses kept on using these words until they *had* to be included in our lexicons. And conversely, when these or any other words such as those that are included in this volume stop being commonly used, they will die and drop out of our dictionary. *You* will determine this, and our lexicographers will have nothing to do with it.

Now by just what methods did such words, for instance, as you have been working with in this book ever get into the dictionary?

This is the way. The technique may be interesting to you.

Somebody writes in and asks the dictionary publisher about an apparently new word, or a staff reader discovers it among the Niagara of words pouring out from the presses of the world. So they first check it to find if it really *is* new. They look for it in all the standard English reference works that have come out during the last two centuries. If they don't find it there, and since it might be foreign, they leaf through glossaries of Sanskrit, Maori, Hansa, Urdu, Hebrew, Afrikaans, and all the languages, ancient and modern, that were spawned by the Tower of Babel. If it still evades them, they take a look at the trade and professional dictionaries, say those of lace-making, politics, petroleum, draperies, botany, and others too numerous to count.

By this time it's a foxy word that's going to fool them!

If the term proves itself as new, they put it on file for about five years.

Now how does it get in?

They watch its *use* by the people during the probationary period. Authors may take it up. Inquiries may come to the office about its meaning. At the end of the interval the record of the neophyte is added up, and *if its score shows a sufficient popular demand,* the word goes in the dictionary. Thus and no otherwise.

Now, how is it *defined?* To be concrete, how were the

definitions of the words in the last chapter originally determined upon?

As the researchers watch a new word in use they copy the actual sentences in which the word appears. When a given dictionary editor finally sits down to make up his definition, he will have in front of him a stack of cards containing sentences that give the word and the context. The meaning, or the meanings, that he gives the word will be based, *not in any way on his own opinion,* but upon the sheaf of popular quotations he finds in front of him. His authority, and the authority of the dictionary, then, lie, not in this editor's particular scholarship, but in *your* whim and in the whim of the other millions who have invented, pronounced, spelled, and defined the word for him.

And so when we study the English language we are studying our own handiwork. It is as democratic as our national institutions, and the so-called "common people" are its inexhaustible source. The final authority for English rests, not with some dictionary House of Lords, but with the House of Commons, and this is what gives our language its vitality, force and rich humanity, and is what helps to make it such a thrilling study.

A "Pop Quiz"

At this point, we are going to challenge you with a surprise test that will give you a yardstick by which you can measure the success you are having in keeping new words in your mind.

We are going to take a single past chapter and see how successfully you've mastered it.

I

Here are the fifteen words from Chapter XII:

lethargy	enervated
nostalgia	ennui
benevolence	vicariously
satiated	misanthrope
frustration	misogynist
weltschmerz	vindictive
antipathy	supercilious
compunction	

123

II

Write each word next to its synonym or synonymous phrase. Some words may be required more than once.

1. Aversion ....
2. Exhausted ....
3. Indirect or second-hand ....
4. Sluggishness ....
5. Tedium ....
6. Weariness of life; sadness for the world ....
7. Remorseful feeling ....
8. Revengeful ....
9. Dislike ....
10. Deprived of vitality ....
11. Longing for the past ....
12. Woman-hater ....
13. Condescending ....
14. Inability to succeed or achieve ....
15. Philosophical and emotional world-sorrow ....
16. Kindheartedness ....
17. Regret for wrongdoing ....
18. Filled full ....

ANSWERS: (1) antipathy; (2) enervated; (3) vicarious; (4) lethargy; (5) ennui; (6) weltschmerz; (7) compunction; (8) vindictiveness; (9) antipathy; (10) enervated; (11) nostalgia; (12) misogynist; (13) supercilious; (14) frustration; (15) weltschmerz; (16) benevolence; (17) compunction; (18) satiated

III

Some of the following statements are false, others are true. Check the correct response.

1. *Misanthropes* have an *antipathy* toward their fellow men.   True...... False......
2. Staying up all night is *enervating*.   True...... False......
3. One can get a *vicarious* thrill from the movies.   True...... False......
4. People full of energy are usually *lethargic*.   True...... False......
5. Young girls are filled with *ennui* at their first party.   True...... False......
6. Optimistic people are weighed down with *weltschmerz*.   True...... False......
7. A military conqueror has strong *compunctions* about taking other people's land.   True...... False......
8. *Vindictiveness* is an exceedingly attractive trait.   True...... False......
9. *Nostalgia* is a prevalent ill among young people who are away from home for the first time.   True...... False......
10. Haters of women are called *misogynists*.   True...... False......
11. The intelligent members of motion-picture audiences have had a *satiety* of bad pictures.   True...... False......
12. The depression generation of the 1930's experienced poignant *frustration*.   True...... False......
13. Adolf Hitler was famous for his great *benevolence*.   True...... False......
14. Modest people are *supercilious*.   True...... False......

ANSWERS: (1) true; (2) true; (3) true; (4) false; (5) false; (6) false; (7) false; (8) false; (9) true; (10) true; (11) true; (12) true; (13) false; (14) false

IV

Here are twelve words and phrases, each one *opposed* in meaning to one of our fifteen words. Can you summon from your mind the word that is *antonymous* to each of the following?

1. Joy in living   ....
2. Exhilaration   ....
3. Chivalry   ....
4. Forgivingness   ....
5. Sympathy   ....
6. First-hand experience   ....
7. Keen interest   ....
8. Heartlessness   ....
9. Hunger   ....
10. Feeling of inferiority   ....
11. Success   ....
12. Malice   ....

ANSWERS: (1) weltschmerz; (2) enervation; (3) misogyny; (4) vindictiveness; (5) antipathy; (6) vicariousness; (7) ennui; (8) compunction; (9) satiety; (10) superciliousness; (11) frustration; (12) benevolence

V

Complete each of the following sentences by one of our fifteen words, or by some form of that word. Not all the words may be required, and some words may be asked for more than once.

1. When I reflect on the pleasant memories of my childhood, I am overcome by a wave of ....

2. Nothing I do is successful; all, all is ....

3. I would have too many .... to deprive him of his one chance of happiness.

4. What is life? What is to be the future of humanity? Shall we all finally destroy one another? I am weighed down with ....

5. No, I don't care to meet that beautiful actress. You forget that I am ....

6. No wonder you are bored and blasé. You are suffering from a .... of pleasure.

7. Oh, I think I shall die if something doesn't happen to relieve my ....

8. You show your superiority too openly. No wonder your friends dislike you and call you ....

9. I have been unable to accomplish anything for the past two years. I seem to have sunk into a state of ....

10. .... have an .... for women.

11. You treat your employees with a pretended generosity and ...., but they see through you and know that you actually have an .... for the working classes.

12. Staying up with that invalid all night has reduced me to a state of ....

13. I bear you no grudge for what you have done. I am not ....

14. I see the motion pictures .... even though I am blind, for my friends come home and tell me all about them.

ANSWERS: (1) nostalgia; (2) frustration; (3) compunctions; (4) weltschmerz; (5) misogynous or misogynistic; (6) satiety; (7) ennui; (8) supercilious; (9) lethargy; (10) misogynists, antipathy; (11) benevolence, antipathy; (12) enervation; (13) vindictive; (14) vicariously

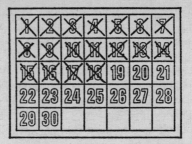

Words About Personalities

Language, most naturally, is an intensely human subject, and all words lead finally to man.

We will turn to terms that deal directly with your friends and with you. Here are twelve words that describe different kinds of personalities.

I
What Kind of Personality Do You Happen to Have?

1. Are you moody, quiet, happy to be alone? Do you spend much of your time thinking of yourself? You are probably an *introvert*.

2. Are you a good mixer? Do you prefer the company of others to solitude? Are you rarely self-conscious and usually more interested in the outside world and in the other fellow than you are in yourself? Would you be apt to make a good salesman? You are probably an *extrovert*.

3. Do you feel that you have some of the qualities listed

in (1) combined with some of those listed in (2)? In common with most people, few of whom are *pure* introverts or extroverts, you are most likely an *ambivert*.

4. Is your mind so selfishly occupied with your own thoughts, desires, opinions, and needs as to make you indifferent to the interests of other folks? You are *egocentric*.

5. Do you often wish to do perfectly innocent, or perhaps not so innocent, things which your Puritan conscience, or your fear of ridicule, or your conservative upbringing, prevents you from doing? You are *inhibited*.

6. Are you so completely lacking in modesty and self-consciousness that you delight in making a spectacle of yourself? Do you make a play for the spotlight and are you eager to put on a one-man show at every gathering? You are an *exhibitionist*.

7. Do you always think of that witty remark *after* you get home? Do you feel that your opinions are not worth expressing? Are you so completely lacking in self-confidence that you rarely achieve the success or recognition that your talents and ability seem to deserve? You are *diffident*.

8. Are you generally sparkling, happy, bubbling over with zest and high spirits? You are *effervescent*.

9. Are you happiest when you are with a crowd? Do you prefer people to solitude and do you feel emotionally most content in the company of friends? You are *gregarious*.

10. Do you walk around with a chip on your shoulder? Are you always ready to do battle? Are you savage, fierce, ruthless, unyielding in your manner and in your arguments? You are *truculent*.

11. Are you grave, gloomy, heavy, foreboding? Do you rarely smile? You are *saturnine*.

12. Are you chivalrous, romantic and idealistic almost to a ridiculous extreme? Are you the opposite of practical? Do you place woman on so high a pedestal that she is unapproachable? Are you always chasing rainbows? You are *quixotic*.

II

To gain firmer control over these words, pronounce them aloud—several times!

1. *introvert* (IN'-trō-vurt')
2. *extrovert* (EKS'-trō-vurt')
3. *ambivert* (AM'-bee-vurt')
4. *egocentric* (ee'-gō-SEN'-trik)
5. *inhibited* (in-HIB'-ə-təd)
6. *exhibitionist* (ek'-sə-BISH'-ə-nist)
7. *diffident* (DIF'-ə-dənt)
8. *effervescent* (ef'-ər-VESS'-ənt)
9. *gregarious* (grə-GAIR'-ee-əs)
10. *truculent* (TRUK'-yə-lənt)
11. *saturnine* (SAT'-ər-nine')
12. *quixotic* (kwik-SOT'-ik)

III

Can you match each word to its definition? Initial letters will guide you. But don't look back, please.

1. Possessed with self-distrust; shy; timid — D ....
2. Bubbly and sparkling in personality — E ....
3. Looking at everything from a personal point of view — E ....
4. Delight with putting on an act in front of others — E ....
5. One whose chief interests are outside of himself and who makes friends easily — E ....
6. Preferring the company of others to solitude — G ....
7. One whose interest is directed inward, who is turned in upon himself, and who is much alone — I ....
8. Idealistic but unpractical — Q ....

9. Morose, gloomy, heavy, dull   S ....
10. Savage and pugnacious in character   T ....
11. One who finds his satisfactions both within and in the outside world   A ....
12. Held back by conscience, early training, fear, feelings of shyness, etc.   I ....

ANSWERS: (1) diffident; (2) effervescent; (3) egocentric; (4) exhibitionist; (5) extrovert; (6) gregarious; (7) introvert; (8) quixotic; (9) saturnine; (10) truculent; (11) ambivert; (12) inhibited

IV

Try once again, without initial letters.
1. Cruel, ferocious   ....
2. Shy and timid   ....
3. Bubbling over   ....
4. Considering self the center of everything   ....
5. Psychically restrained   ....
6. One who loves to be the center of attention   ....
7. One whose interests are directed outward   ....
8. Liking to be with other people   ....
9. One whose interest is directed inward   ....
10. Idealistic but impractical   ....
11. Gloomy and morose   ....
12. One who finds his satisfactions both inside and outside himself   ....

ANSWERS: (1) truculent; (2) diffident; (3) effervescent; (4) egocentric; (5) inhibited; (6) exhibitionist; (7) extrovert; (8) gregarious; (9) introvert; (10) quixotic; (11) saturnine; (12) ambivert

V

Nouns often end in such characteristic suffixes as *-tion* or *-sion, -ism, -ence, -ness,* and *-ity.* Can you figure out the noun form of each adjective?

1. *introverted* (as in: characterized by ....)
2. *extroverted* (as in: known for his ....)
3. *ambiverted* (as in: most people tend toward ....)
4. *egocentric* (as in: hated for his annoying ....)
5. *inhibited* (as in: a prey to oppressive ....)
6. *exhibitionistic* (as in: accused of ....)
7. *diffident* (as in: projects a poor image because of his ....)
8. *effervescent* (as in: delighted with his charm and ....)
9. *gregarious* (as in: a slave to his unending ....)
10. *truculent* (as in: cowed everyone with his ....)
11. *quixotic* (as in: such ridiculous ....)
12. *saturnine* (as in: oppressed by ....)

ANSWERS: (1) introversion;   (2) extroversion;   (3) ambiversion;   (4) egocentricity *or* egocentrism;   (5) inhibitedness *or* inhibition;   (6) exhibitionism;   (7) diffidence;   (8) effervescence; (9) gregariousness;   (10) truculence;   (11) quixoticism;   (12) saturninity (sat'-ər-NIN'-ə-tee)

With each chapter, your power over words is growing. And yet you are doing much more than merely learning lists of words. In addition to the new words you have learned, you have also opened up new avenues of thought for yourself. An improved vocabulary leads to enlarged horizons, new vistas, experience with ideas not previously experienced. It is no accident that successful and intelligent people have the largest vocabularies. Their competence with words is a token, a result, of their breadth of thinking and experience.

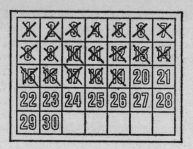

Adjectives
Give You Power

A vocabulary of power gives you the ability to condense a highly involved thought into a single word. Thus, if you wish to describe an action that is so ordinary and undistinguished and common that it immediately marks its perpetrator as a person completely lacking in imagination (notice how many words we have used to express this thought), you will use the word *plebeian*. On the other hand, an act that indicates excessive desire to be overattentive, with attendant evidence of insincerity and a suspicion of ulterior motives, might be characterized as *obsequious*. Again, an action that is sickeningly sentimental and indicative of emotional immaturity, and one that is often accompanied by tears, could be called *maudlin*.

I

There are many such words that compress a wealth of meaning and emotion into a few syllables. Note how expressive the following phrases are:

1. A *plebeian* (plǝ-BEE'-ǝn) outlook on life
2. *Obsequious* (ob-SEE'-kwee-ǝs) attentions of the headwaiter
3. A *maudlin* (MAWD'-lin) motion picture
4. A *perfunctory* (pǝr-FUNK'-tǝ-ree) examination by a busy doctor who has very little time for you
5. An *abortive* (ǝ-BAWR'-tiv) attempt to gain his ends
6. A *surreptitious* (sur'-rep-TISH'-ǝs) movement on the part of the thief
7. A *presumptuous* (prǝ-ZUMP'-choo-ǝs) question to put to the Governor
8. The *sadistic* (sǝ-DISS'-tik) treatment of the prisoner by ruthless guards
9. A *flagrant* (FLAY'-grǝnt) misuse of company funds
10. An *inane* (in-AYN') remark

II

From an analysis of the phrases you have just studied, write each word next to its definition:

1. Openly, glaringly wrong or scandalous ....
2. Senseless; silly; empty ....
3. Made foolish by liquor; tearfully affectionate or sentimental ....
4. Overcourteous and servile in manner ....
5. Done mechanically and without interest; superficial and careless ....
6. Unduly confident or bold; audacious; arrogant; taking too much for granted ....
7. Inclined to cruelty; getting pleasure out of hurting others ....
8. By secret or stealthy means ....
9. Common; coarse; vulgarly ordinary, mediocre, or commonplace ....
10. Coming to naught; failing ....

ANSWERS: (1) flagrant;   (2) inane;   (3) maudlin;

(4) obsequious; (5) perfunctory; (6) presumptuous; (7) sadistic; (8) surreptitious; (9) plebeian; (10) abortive

III

Try the same method with another list of valuable and expressive adjectives.

1. *Wanton* (WAHN'-tən) cruelty
2. *Crass* (KRASS') behavior
3. *Macabre* (mə-KAH'-bər) mystery
4. *Dogmatic* (dog-MAT'-ik) assertion
5. *Vitriolic* (vit'-ree-OL'-ik) satire
6. *Intermittent* (in-tər-MIT'-ənt) ringing of the telephone
7. *Subversive* (səb-VUR'-siv) activities of people who wish to overthrow the government
8. *Desultory* (DESS'-əl-taw'-ree) flitting from one subject to another
9. A *sardonic* (sahr-DON'-ik) smile

IV

Again, from an analysis of the phrases in Section III, write each word next to its definition.

1. Passing irregularly from one thing to another; changeable; without method or plan   ....
2. Descriptive of an opinion stated in an overpositive and arrogant manner   ....
3. Recklessly inconsiderate or heartless; unrestrained; extravagant   ....
4. Stupid in a grossly inconsiderate way   ....
5. Ceasing and starting again   ....
6. Bitter, scornful, and sneering   ....
7. Pertaining to, indicative of, or suggest-

ing death; hence, gruesome, grim, ghastly, horrible   ....

8. Extremely biting or sarcastic; figuratively
caustic or bitter   ....

9. Tending to overthrow from the very
foundations, as of a moral or political
force; aiming to destroy   ....

ANSWERS: (1) desultory; (2) dogmatic; (3) wanton;
(4) crass; (5) intermittent; (6) sardonic;
(7) macabre; (8) vitriolic; (9) subversive

V

You will recall from the previous chapter that a noun
often and characteristically ends in such suffixes as *-ity*
(*saturninity*), *-ness* (*gregariousness*), *-ion* (*inhibition*),
-ism (*asceticism*), *-ence* (*diffidence*), *-ance* (*circum-
stance*), *-ency* or *-ancy* (*potency, occupancy*), etc.

Adverbs end in *-ly*, as *diffidently, gregariously,* etc.

Can you change each adjective as required below?

1. *Obsequious* to a noun: "His .... was annoying."

2. *Perfunctory* to an adverb: "He did his work
..............."

3. *Surreptitious* to an adverb: "He crept through the
house ...."

4. *Presumptuous* to a noun: "Your .... will be
punished."

5. *Sadistic* to a noun denoting the person: "He is
a ...."

6. *Sadistic* to a noun denoting the philosophy: "He
was a victim of his wife's ...."

7. *Flagrant* to a noun: "I cannot understand how you
can break the law with such ...."

8. *Inane* to a plural noun: "His speech is full of
................."

9. *Wanton* to an adverb: "................, she broke her husband's heart."
10. *Crass* to a noun: "His .... makes it impossible for him to be accepted by refined people."
11. *Dogmatic* to a noun: "Why do you always speak with such ....?"
12. *Intermittent* to an adverb: "The rain came down ...."
13. *Desultory* to an adverb: "He works ...."

ANSWERS: (1) obsequiousness;   (2) perfunctorily;   (3) surreptitiously;   (4) presumption *or* presumptuousness;   (5) sadist;   (6) sadism;   (7) flagrancy;   (8) inanities;   (9) wantonly; (10) crassness *or* crassitude;   (11) dogmatism *or* dogmaticness;   (12) intermittently; (13) desultorily

VI

First, review all nineteen words carefully (including their noun and adverb forms), pronouncing them aloud once again to fix them in your mind. Then complete each of the following sentences with one of the words or forms that you think will fit best.

1. He made an .... attempt to regain the governorship; his defeat left him a sad and bitter man who thereafter spoke .... of his political past.
2. Can you think of anything quite so .... cruel as war?
3. Pompous people delight in .... attendance on their every wish.
4. Thievery will out, and anything you do .... will some day be found out.
5. Please don't state so .... that democracy is a fiasco. Time will show the stupidity of such a statement.

6. He disliked his job heartily, and therefore it was no surprise that he discharged his duties so ....

7. With what malicious and .... satisfaction the prosecutor made the witness reveal his past!

8. Read with a purpose; .... reading is neither satisfactory nor sensible.

9. During a political campaign, candidates often descend to making .... attacks on their opponents.

10. It was an overcast day, with only .... sunshine.

11. This error is so glaring and .... that I'm amazed you didn't catch it.

12. Isn't it rather .... for a person of your reputation to ask to be my friend?

13. He has a .... tongue; his biting sarcasm has alienated everyone who knows him.

14. Peaceful people are aghast at the .... destruction of life and property that occurs during wars and riots.

15. He made a futile, ... attempt at rescue.

16. Such .... materialism will never lead to real happiness.

ANSWERS: (1) abortive, sardonically; (2) wantonly; (3) obsequious; (4) surreptitiously; (5) dogmatically; (6) perfunctorily; (7) sadistic; (8) desultory; (9) flagrant, inane, wanton, crass, or vitriolic; (10) intermittent; (11) flagrant; (12) presumptuous; (13) vitriolic; (14) wanton; (15) abortive; (16) crass

The answers given above are not necessarily the only possible ones. In some of the sentences several of the words will fit. As a person whose vocabulary is becoming daily larger and larger, you realize that there are a multitude of ways of saying the same thing. But the particular word you choose will determine the flavor of your thought. This is the priceless value of a large vocabulary. Out of

your wide range of words you can pick and choose the
exact term that will best express each subtle nuance in
your mind.

VII

Now a quick and final run-through to reinforce your
learning. Is each pair of words nearly the *same* or more
nearly *opposed* in meaning?

1. *plebeian*	unusual	Same......	Opposed......
2. *obsequious*	brusque	Same......	Opposed......
3. *maudlin*	sentimental	Same......	Opposed......
4. *perfunctory*	superficial	Same......	Opposed......
5. *abortive*	successful	Same......	Opposed......
6. *surreptitious*	aboveboard	Same......	Opposed......
7. *presumptu-ous*	humble	Same......	Opposed......
8. *sadistic*	cruel	Same......	Opposed......
9. *flagrant*	hidden	Same......	Opposed......
10. *inane*	meaningful	Same......	Opposed......
11. *wanton*	restrained	Same......	Opposed......
12. *crass*	refined	Same......	Opposed......
13. *macabre*	eerie	Same......	Opposed......
14. *dogmatic*	opinionated	Same......	Opposed......
15. *vitriolic*	sarcastic	Same......	Opposed......
16. *intermittent*	continuous	Same......	Opposed......
17. *subversive*	protective	Same......	Opposed......
18. *desultory*	aimless	Same......	Opposed......
19. *sardonic*	bitter	Same......	Opposed......

ANSWERS: (1) opposed; (2) opposed; (3) same;
(4) same; (5) opposed; (6) opposed;
(7) opposed; (8) same; (9) opposed;
(10) opposed; (11) opposed; (12) opposed; (13) same; (14) same; (15)
same; (16) opposed; (17) opposed; (18)
same; (19) same

Learning Words the Modern Way

This book is not a memory course.

Merely memorizing lists of words by rote happens to be the slowest and most difficult way to remember them. If you follow such a routine you will find that you have forgotten most of the list by the next day.

What, then, is the correct procedure?

Just this.

Look at the word first, if you can, in its context: in the paragraph where it appears. The very sense of the paragraph will give you an inkling of the significance of the word—even if you have never seen it before. You naturally become eager to know the definition of the word in order to understand the sentence pattern in which you have seen it. Your approach, then, is *indirect and psychological,* because you wish the information, not as an end in itself, but as a means to an end. You realize that if you learn the meaning of the word you will comprehend the meaning of the sentence. You are using what is called the modern *inductive* method, in that you first discover the word at work, you are challenged by it, you guess at its meaning, and you then confirm or correct your guess by referring to the dictionary.

When you use this method, the words are no longer so much dead wood, to be piled up in your mind, but are living entities, charged with action and emotion. They then become hard to forget.

Let's be specific and illustrate our point.

We will discuss thirteen adverbs and two adverbial phrases and try to prove how much easier it is to learn by the *indirect, inductive, and psychological* route.

I

Give your careful attention to the following sentences in Groups A, B, C, D, and E. In each sentence you will find an adverb in italics. If the word is new to you, try to guess at its meaning.

GROUP A

1. He complained *acrimoniously*.
2. We argued *acrimoniously*.
3. They mocked each other *acrimoniously*.
   (You can feel the unpleasant overtone of this word, can't you?)

GROUP B

1. He completed the operation *adroitly*.
2. He drove *adroitly* through the maze of traffic.
3. *Adroitly* she knitted the complicated stitch.
   (This word obviously applies to some manual action.)

GROUP C

1. He moved slowly and *circumspectly* through the range of fire.
2. Fearing a trick, he answered all questions *circumspectly*.

3. By walking *circumspectly* he avoided an ambush.
   (There's a feeling of watchfulness about this word.)

GROUP D

1. These two building leases run *concomitantly*.
2. Living and learning go on *concomitantly*.
3. Rain, snow, and sleet, all came down *concomitantly*.
   (You probably know why two or more things *must*
   be involved in these actions, even if you happen
   never to have seen the word before.)

GROUP E

1. He examined the plans *cursorily*.
2. He ran through the pages *cursorily,* then threw the
   novel down in disgust.
3. He did his homework so *cursorily* that he flunked his
   examination.
   (This word should carry an impression of superficial haste.)

II

Now pronounce the words aloud.
1. *acrimoniously* (ak'-rə-MŌ'-nee-əs-lee)
2. *adroitly* (ə-DROYT'-lee)
3. *circumspectly* (sur'-kəm-SPEKT'-lee)
4. *concomitantly* (kon-KOM'-ə-tənt-lee)
5. *cursorily* (KUR'-sə-rə-lee)

III

Let us try five more words, using the same intriguing
and productive method. Again, try to figure out the prob-
able meanings of the italicized words.
1. Teachers are apt to talk *didactically*.
2. Extremely modest persons usually speak of their own
   accomplishments *disparagingly*.

3. People with extremely facile and ready tongues can talk *glibly*.
4. The person who is looking for sympathy talks *plaintively*.
5. Pessimists usually speak *ominously* of the future.

IV

Pronounce them:
1. *didactically* (dy'-DAK'-tik-lee)
2. *disparagingly* (dis-PAIR'-ə-jing-ly)
3. *glibly* (GLIB'-lee)
4. *plaintively* (PLAIN'-tiv-lee)
5. *ominously* (OM'-ə-nəs-lee)

V

And still another five, in the same way.
1. Man cannot break the laws of nature with *impunity*.
2. He placed his hand on the hot radiator *inadvertently*.
3. He was a disagreeable old man who answered every question *irascibly*.
4. Inasmuch as the plans were executed *sub rosa,* the stockholders realized too late how completely they had been defrauded.
5. He never gave up quietly. He always complained *vociferously* if he thought he had been treated unfairly.

VI

Pronounce them:
1. *impunity* (im-PYOO'-nə-tee)
2. *inadvertently* (in-ad-VUR'-tənt-lee)
3. *irascibly* (eye-RASS'-ə-blee)

4. *sub rosa* (sub-RŌ′-zə)
5. *vociferously* (vō-SIF′-ə-rəs-lee)

VII

O.K. You have looked at, thought about, and tried to understand fifteen useful adverbial expressions. Now take the next step in the learning process: *write* the word (or phrase) in the blank line next to its definition. Initial letters are offered as guides.

1. Expertly; dexterously; with skillful use of the hands or mind   A ....
2. Accompanying; occurring together   C ....
3. In the fashion of a teacher; as if teaching a lesson   D ....
4. In a manner of smooth ease and fluency; without hesitation   G ....
5. In a heedless manner; without care; inattentively   I ....
6. Forebodingly; in a way portending evil   O ....
7. In strict confidence; privately   S ....
8. In a loud-voiced manner; vehemently; noisily   V ....
9. Expressing sadness or melancholy   P ....
10. Angrily; irritably; in hot-tempered fashion   I ....
11. With freedom from punishment or injurious consequences   with I ....
12. Speaking slightingly of, in a way to undervalue and discredit   D ....
13. Hastily and superficially, without due care and attention   C ....
14. Cautiously with watchfulness in all directions   C ....
15. With sharpness and bitterness of speech or temper   A ....

ANSWERS: (1) adroitly; (2) concomitantly; (3) didactically; (4) glibly; (5) inadvertently; (6)
ominously; (7) sub rosa; (8) vociferously;
(9) plaintively; (10) irascibly; (11) with
impunity; (12) disparagingly; (13) cursorily; (14) circumspectly; (15) acrimoniously

VIII

Next, you reinforce your learning even more. Here are
forty-six synonyms or synonymous phrases that fit the
thirteen adverbs and two adverbial phrases you have been
working on. Each adverb or adverbial phrase will be required two or more times. Can you go through this
exercise happily, smoothly, and with an increasing sense of
confidence and power? You are on your own, with no
initial letters to help you.

1. hastily   ....
2. warily   ....
3. in a teacher-like manner   ....
4. irritably   ....
5. in a way foreboding evil   ....
6. sadly   ....
7. in a hidden manner   ....
8. loudly   ....
9. inauspiciously   ....
10. angrily   ....
11. dexterously   ....
12. cautiously   ....
13. slightingly   ....
14. fluently   ....
15. caustically   ....
16. heedlessly   ....
17. at the same time   ....
18. with anger and annoyance   ....
19. prudently   ....
20. with exemption from punishment ....
21. smoothly   ....

22. stingingly ....
23. thoughtlessly ....
24. deprecatingly ....
25. conjointly ....
26. without danger of punishment ....
27. bitterly ....
28. unhesitatingly ....
29. depreciatively ....
30. skillfully ....
31. irately ....
32. in a way expressing coming danger or misfortune ....
33. sorrowfully ....
34. without incurring penalty, harm, or loss ....
35. rapidly and hastily ....
36. like an instructor ....
37. mournfully ....
38. secretly ....
39. clamorously ....
40. in loud tones ....
41. noisily ....
42. instructively ....
43. confidentially ....
44. in a melancholy way ....
45. belittlingly ....
46. superficially ....

ANSWERS: (1) cursorily; (2) circumspectly; (3) didactically; (4) irascibly; (5) ominously; (6) plaintively; (7) sub rosa; (8) vociferously; (9) ominously; (10) irascibly; (11) adroitly; (12) circumspectly; (13) disparagingly; (14) glibly; (15) acrimoniously; (16) inadvertently; (17) concomitantly; (18) irascibly; (19) circumspectly; (20) with impunity; (21) glibly; (22) acrimoniously; (23) inadvertently; (24) disparagingly; (25) concomitantly; (26) with impunity; (27) acrimoniously; (28) glibly; (29) disparagingly; (30) adroitly; (31) irascibly; (32) ominously; (33) plaintively; (34) with impunity; (35) cursorily; (36) didactically; (37) plaintively; (38) sub rosa; (39) vociferously; (40) vociferously; (41) vociferously; (42) didactically; (43) sub rosa; (44) plaintively; (45) disparagingly; (46) cursorily

IX

Find an adverb or adverbial phrase that will best fit each of the seven situations described below.

1. You are a burglar. You have just entered a wealthy home through an unlocked window. All is dark, and alas, you have forgotten to bring your searchlight with you. To add to your troubles, you can't find the electric switch. How will you move around in this room until you can get your bearings? ....

2. You are an irritable, touchy old man, and as you walk along the street on this cold, raw morning you feel nothing but enmity toward the whole world. A beggar stops you for a coin. How do you refuse? ....

3. A friend has been importuning you for weeks to look over a novel he is writing and give him your criticism. Knowing your friend you are certain that the novel is bad even before you read it; besides, you are a very busy man. Rather than give your friend a blunt refusal, however, you take the manuscript home one evening. How do you examine it?
....

4. Your small son wishes to know why it snows. You are well versed in the natural sciences and have made it a habit to answer all your son's questions as clearly and accurately as possible. How do you answer him? ....

5. You have influence with the chief of police, and furthermore, your wife is the mayor's daughter. Consequently, you never trouble to obey traffic laws. In fact, you can break them ....

6. A woman has broken your heart purposely, and with malice aforethought. She has left you a disillusioned man. It takes you years even to begin to get over it. And then one day you meet her again. She is gay, debonaire; she has obviously forgotten what she has done to you. This angers you and you intend to sting her when you remind her. In what fashion do you speak to her? ....

7. You are a very modest person. Rather than praise anything you have done, you prefer to take as little credit as possible for your accomplishments. How do you usually speak of yourself? ....

ANSWERS: (1) circumspectly; (2) irascibly; (3) cursorily; (4) didactically; (5) with impunity; (6) acrimoniously; (7) disparagingly

X

An important step in improving your vocabulary is to practice changing parts of speech. Drop the *-ly* of the thirteen adverbs and you have adjectives; choose the proper suffix (*-ness, -ion, -ence, -ance, -ism, -ity*) and you can form a noun from the adjective.

By the way, two noun endings we have not yet discussed will be required in this exercise, *-ony* (as in *ceremony* from the adjective *ceremonious*) and *-ment* (as in *development* from the adjective *developing*).

Ready to turn adverbs into nouns?

1. *acrimoniously* ....
2. *adroitly* ....
3. *circumspectly* ....
4. *concomitantly* ....
5. *cursorily* ....

6. *didactically* ....
7. *disparagingly* ....
8. *glibly* ....
9. *plaintively* ....
10. *ominously* ....
11. *inadvertently* ....
12. *irascibly* ....
13. *vociferously* ....

ANSWERS: (1) acrimony; (2) adroitness; (3) circum-
spection; (4) concomitance; (5) cursori-
ness; (6) didacticism; (7) disparagement;
(8) glibness; (9) plaintiveness; (10) omi-
nousness; (11) inadvertence; (12) irasci-
bility; (13) vociferousness

Most adjectives can be made into nouns by adding
-*ness,* although this is not always the most sophisticated
suffix. Therefore, alternate forms for 1, 3, 4, 6, 7, 11, and
12 are *acrimoniousness, circumspectness, concomitantness*
(not the happiest of choices), *didacticness, disparagingness*
(again, awkward), *inadvertentness* (awkward), and *iras-
cibleness.*

Occasionally you may feel that these exercises are time-
consuming. But we urge you never to let the lack of time
stand as an obstacle to this work. Thomas Carlyle, the
great philosopher, claimed that there is time in every
man's life for a career within a career. Even so-called
geniuses are geniuses largely because they are willing to
use the time that others throw away. It was Michelangelo
who said: "If people only knew how hard I work to gain
my mastery it wouldn't seem so wonderful at all." And
Alexandre Dumas, the transcendent French novelist, con-
fessed: "Infatuated, half through conceit, half through love
of my art, I achieve the impossible working as none else
ever works. . . ."

Careers are not had by wishing and hoping. They are
bought with work and enthusiasm.

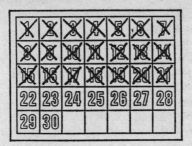

Words from Latin

A large part of our English vocabulary, as we know, derives from Latin. This language is no longer used except in the somewhat modified form of "Church Latin." Old Latin was no longer a spoken tongue when modern English began; yet English is such a vital and avid tongue that it has steadily fed upon Latin, and even today this Roman speech is constantly taken over into English by scholars, philologists, and scientists.

Any time you run an inquisitive plow through our language you turn up Latin roots everywhere.

I

There is the simple word *animal.* Why particularly do we use the word *animal* instead of some other combination of syllables?

Animal is from Latin *anima,* "mind," "breath," "soul," or "spirit," and of course, animals, as opposed to minerals or *inanimate* objects, do breathe and do possess that mysterious something that gives them a life not found in "inanimate" things. The root *anima* is found in a host of common English words:

*anima*lcule—a tiny live thing

*anima*te—to breathe life into

equ*anim*ity—equal or placid spirit or mind

magn*anim*ous—of large, or noble, spirit

un*anim*ous—of one mind

in*anima*te—without a soul; hence, not alive

*anim*osity—vehement enmity: literally, with one's mind against

pusill*anim*ous—fainthearted; cowardly: literally, of small mind

*anima*dvert—to turn the mind to; to notice; to criticize

II

In many cases, English words are formed by combining parts of two or more Latin words. Thus "equanimity" is a fusion of *aequus,* "equal," and *anima.* You will recognize the root *aequus* (spelled *equ-* or *-iqu* in English) in such words as *equation, equality, equity, iniquity. Magnanimous* combines *magnus,* "large," with *anima.* Engage in a little etymological exploration, if you will, and see what other words you can turn up with the stem of *magnus,* "large."

1. .... A person large in importance, as in an industry
2. .... To make large
3. .... Splendor; grandeur
4. .... Speaking big or in pompous or flowery style
5. .... Bigness or greatness
6. .... A large bottle (two quarts) for champagne or other wine
7. .... A great work; a literary or artistic work of importance

ANSWERS: (1) magnate; (2) magnify; (3) magnificence; (4) magniloquent; (5) magnitude; (6) magnum; (7) magnum opus

III

Let us pronounce the words we have discovered so far.
For best results, say them aloud several times.

1. *animalcule* (AN'-ə-məl-kyool')
2. *animate,* verb: (AN'-ə-mayt')
    adjective: (AN'-ə-mət)
3. *equanimity* (ee'-kwə-NIM'-ə-tee)
4. *magnanimous* (mag-NAN'-ə-məs)
5. *unanimous* (yoo-NAN'-ə-məs)
6. *inanimate* (in-AN'-ə-mət)
7. *animosity* (an'-ə-MOS'-ə-tee)
8. *pusillanimous* (pyoo'-sə-LAN'-ə-məs)
9. *animadvert* (AN'-ə-məd-vert')
10. *magnate* (MAG'-nayt)
11. *magnify* (MAG'-nə-fy)
12. *magnificence* (mag-NIF'-ə-sənce)
13. *magniloquent* (mag-NIL'-ə-kwənt)
14. *magnitude* (MAG'-nə-tood')
15. *magnum* (MAG'-nəm)
16. *magnum opus* (MAGH'-nəm-O'-pəs)

IV

Now, to give you practice in spelling these words and to
reinforce your learning, we ask you to write the word that
fits each definition.

1. Large-minded; not petty   M ....
2. Small-minded; cowardly   P ....
3. Strong hostility   A ....
4. To invest with life   A ....
5. Make larger   M ....
6. Without life   I ....
7. Turn one's mind to   A ....
8. Agreed to by everyone   U ....
9. Using flowery language   M ....

10. Placid, unruffled temper-
    ament   E ....

11. Great literary or artistic
    work   M .... O ....

12. Two-quart bottle   M ....

13. Largeness; large size   M ....

14. Greatness; grandeur   M ....

15. Important person in
    industry   M ....

16. Very small creature   A ....

ANSWERS: (1) magnanimous; (2) pusillanimous; (3)
         animosity; (4) animate; (5) magnify;
         (6) inanimate; (7) animadvert; (8) unani-
         mous; (9) magniloquent; (10) equanimity;
         (11) magnum opus; (12) magnum; (13)
         magnitude; (14) magnificence; (15) mag-
         nate; (16) animalcule

∨

Unanimous combines *unus,* "one," with *anima,* "mind."
Can you think of some other English words which contain
unus?

1. .... Make into one

2. .... A fabulous animal with a single, straight
                   horn

3. .... Of one form or kind

4. .... The state of being united

5. .... Descriptive of the only one of its kind

6. .... Harmony; also, a joining together in
                   sound

7. .... A single one

ANSWERS: (1) unify or unite; (2) unicorn; (3) uni-
         form; (4) union, unity, or unification; (5)
         unique; (6) unison; (7) unit

VI

Pronounce the new words:
1. *unify* (YŌŌ'-nə-fy')
2. *unite* (yōō-NITE')
3. *unicorn* (YŌŌ'-nə-kawrn)
4. *uniform* (YŌŌ'-nə-fawrm)
5. *union* (YŌŌN'-yən)
6. *unity* (YŌŌ'-nə-tee)
7. *unification* (yōō-nə-fə-KAY'-shən)
8. *unique* (yōō-NEEK')
9. *unison* (YŌŌ'-nə-sən)
10. *unit* (YŌŌ'-nit)

VII

Continuing our etymological exploration, let us next consider the word *benevolence*. Its meaning—"a feeling of good will toward others" or "a charitable action for the benefit of others"—can be understood better when we analyze the two Latin roots that have been welded together to form the word: *bene*, "well," and *volens*, "wishing." Benevolence means, literally, "wishing others well." *Bene* is found in other words. Here are a few:

 *bene*fit *bene*ficiary *bene*diction *bene*factor

The root *volens*, "wishing," also appears frequently:

  *vol*ition *vol*untary *vol*unteer

If we now dissect two of the words containing *bene*, we will discover that new Latin roots can easily be added to our repertoire; *benediction*, "a blessing," is, literally, a "saying well." The root *dic* is from Latin *dicere*, "to say" or "to tell." You can see it in the following words:

 *dic*tate *dic*taphone *dic*tion male*dic*tion in*dict*
       pre*dict*

Again, *benefactor*, literally "well-doer," contains the Latin *facere*, "to do" or "to make." Watch how this root is employed in the following words.

*factor   factory   manu*fact*ure   *fact   *factotum
*factual

VIII

Thus, the study of a few of these simple words brings to light eight new roots. Here are the Latin roots with their meanings. Can you recall an English word using each root?

ROOT	MEANING	EXAMPLE
1. *anima*	soul, spirit, mind	....
2. *aequus*	even, equal	....
3. *magnus*	large, big, great	....
4. *unus*	one, single	....
5. *bene*	well	....
6. *volens*	wishing	....
7. *facere*	to do, to make	....
8. *dicere*	to say, to tell	....

IX

Can you recall the other Greek and Latin roots that you have learned in previous chapters? In the chart below you will find a list of them, each with an example. Can you fill in the English meaning of each root?

ROOT	EXAMPLE	MEANING
1. *monos*	*monocle*	....
2. *bis*	*bicycle*	....
3. *polys*	*polygamy*	....
4. *misein*	*misogyny*	....
5. *gamos*	*bigamy*	....
6. *theos*	*monotheism*	....
7. *anthropos*	*anthropology*	....
8. *philein*	*philatelist*	....
9. *logos*	*philology*	....
10. *cuspis*	*bicuspid*	....
11. *glotta*	*polyglot*	....

ANSWERS: (1) one;   (2) twice, two;   (3) many;   (4) to hate;   (5) marriage;   (6) God;   (7) man; (8) to love;   (9) study of, word;   (10) point;   (11) tongue

You will find it excellent practice to keep a weather eye out for these roots and for their various and varied combinations in your daily reading. There are so many of them that it becomes a fascinating sport to try to trace them. There is the Latin word *signum,* or "sign," which gives us in*sign*ia, the signs you wear; *sign*al, a sign; *sign*ify, make a sign; and such others as de*sign,* *sign*ature, in*sign*ificant. We also have the Latin *portare,* "to carry," which leads to *port*er, one who carries; *port*able, able to be carried; re*port*er, one who carries news back; de*port,* carry away; im*port,* carry in; and ex*port,* carry out.

A knowledge of Latin and Greek roots is a splendid vocabulary stretcher.

Test Your Progress

There is one thing that we cannot overemphasize in this daily word study, and that is the high importance of continually reviewing the work that you have done. New words that come into your vocabulary are as elusive as little shining eels, and unless you rehearse them constantly you will find that they will wriggle out from between your mental fingers and slip back into the sea of language.

If you want to make swift progress, take each page of this book seriously, review your work as a matter of course, and so secure the ground as you proceed.

Here is another hint. Be sure to finish this book. Forty-nine out of fifty persons don't thoroughly finish what they begin. This is what will make success so easy for you. Use your will power. Will power is often just another name for courage. Perseverance is energy made habitual. And perseverance, continuously applied, may become genius. So don't just finish this book—or this chapter—and lay it aside. Put it to work. Too many people are forever learning and never doing.

Right now we are going to challenge you with a review of Chapters X to XXI. The tests that follow will not be easy, for they are intended to show up any weak spots in your methods of study.

I

Match the descriptions in Column B to the words in Column A.

	A.		B.
1.	*atheist*	a.	Loud-mouthed woman
2.	*virtuoso*	b.	Connoisseur of good food
3.	*virago*	c.	Disbeliever in God
4.	*gourmet*	d.	Beginner
5.	*tyro*	e.	One who leads an austere life
6.	*philatelist*	f.	Stamp-collector
7.	*ascetic*	g.	Traitor
8.	*pedant*	h.	Boot-licker
9.	*judas*	i.	Skilled practitioner of the arts
10.	*sycophant*	j.	One who is ostentatious about his learning

II

Write the word with the indicated initial letter that satisfies each definition.

1.	Insane desire to set fires	P ....
2.	Uncontrollable propensity to steal	K ....
3.	Forgetfulness of the past	A ....
4.	Sleepwalking	S ....
5.	Alternating fits of despondency and hilarity	M ....
6.	Split personality	S ....
7.	Fear of closed spaces	C ....
8.	Continuous drunkenness	D ....
9.	Persecution complex	P ....
10.	Fear of large spaces	A ....

III

Choose the word in group A that satisfies each of the definitions in Group B.

A   lethargy   weltschmerz   superciliousness
    nostalgia   antipathy   vindictiveness
    benevolence   compunction   misogyny
    satiety   enervation   misanthropy
    frustration   ennui   vicariousness

B   1. Homesickness ....
    2. Good will to all ....
    3. Repletion ....
    4. Thwarting ....
    5. Dislike ....
    6. World-sorrow ....
    7. Hatred of women ....
    8. Scruple ....
    9. Revengefulness ....
   10. Haughtiness ....
   11. Sluggishness ....
   12. Exhaustion ....
   13. Boredom ....
   14. Hatred of mankind ....
   15. Indirect experience ....

IV

Write in the science that deals with each of the following subjects. The initial letter is given.

1. Mankind   A .... logy
2. Rocks   G .... logy
3. Ancient relics   A .... logy
4. Unborn babies   E .... logy
5. Insects   E .... logy
6. Distribution of races   E .... logy
7. Derivation of words   E .... logy

8. Birds   *O* .... *logy*
9. Languages   *P* .... *logy*
10. The human mind   *P* .... *logy*

V

Here are two columns of ten words each. Where the words opposite each other are synonyms, write the letter "S" between the pair. Where they have opposite meanings, write "O." Where the words have no relationship to each other, write "N."

1. *loquacious*   ....   talkative
2. *gullible*   ....   shrewd
3. *suave*   ....   happy
4. *pompous*   ....   conceited
5. *taciturn*   ....   silent
6. *phlegmatic*   ....   excitable
7. *erudite*   ....   ignorant
8. *complacent*   ....   constant
9. *punctilious*   ....   careless
10. *indefatigable*   ....   tireless

VI

In column A are ten definitions; in column B are ten blanks, each with an initial and final letter. The definitions in column A and the words to be supplied in column B do not necessarily face each other. It is up to you to unscramble the columns and fill in the remaining letters of each word. For instance, start with number 1, "minor indiscretion." Now run down column B and see if (with the initial and last letters to guide you) you can recall the word that the phrase "minor indiscretion" describes. When you succeed in remembering it, fill it in.

A.   B.
1. minor indiscretion   1. P .... y
2. poverty   2. M .... r

3. boastfulness	3. J	.... m
4. cure-all	4. B	.... o
5. failure	5. P	.... a
6. characteristic peculiarity	6. P	.... o
7. irregularity	7. F	.... o
8. warmongering	8. A	.... y
9. pretend illness	9. C	.... y
10. trickery	10. I	.... y

VII

Match the two columns.

A.	B.
1. one whose mind is turned inward	a. *diffident*
2. self-centered	b. *extrovert*
3. restrained	c. *inhibited*
4. modest	d. *saturnine*
5. bubbling over with high spirits	e. *egocentric*
6. company-loving	f. *quixotic*
7. fierce; overbearing	g. *introvert*
8. gloomy	h. *effervescent*
9. extravagantly chivalrous	i. *truculent*
10. one whose mind is turned outward	j. *gregarious*

VIII

In each of the five lines below there is one word that correctly expresses the meaning given in the word or words in italics just ahead. Check a, b, or c.

1. *common, ordinary:* a. plebeian, b. obsequious, c. maudlin
2. *miserably failing:* a. perfunctory, b. abortive, c. surreptitious
3. *cruel:* a. presumptuous, b. sadistic, c. flagrant
4. *vulgar:* a. inane, b. wanton, c. crass
5. *biting:* a. macabre, b. dogmatic, c. vitriolic

IX

Proceed as in Test VIII.
1. *at the same time:* a. acrimoniously, b. adroitly, c. concomitantly
2. *carefully:* a. circumspectly, b. cursorily, c. didactically
3. *smoothly:* a. disparagingly, b. glibly, c. plaintively
4. *threateningly:* a. ominously, b. with impunity, c. inadvertently
5. *secretly:* a. irascibly, b. sub rosa, c. vociferously

X

Write the English meaning of each italicized Greek or Latin root.
1. *magn*animous ....
2. *uni*que ....
3. un*anim*ous ....
4. *bene*fit ....
5. ~~*bene*volence~~ ....
6. *dict*aphone ....
7. manu*fact*ure ....
8. mono*gamy* ....
9. *theo*logy ....
10. *bi*cycle ....

ANSWERS: I: (1) c;   (2) i;   (3) a;   (4) b;   (5) d;   (6) f;   (7) e; (8) j;   (9) g;   (10) h

II: (1) pyromania;   (2) kleptomania;   (3) amnesia;   (4) somnambulism;   (5) manic-depression;   (6) schizophrenia;   (7) claustrophobia; (8) dipsomania;   (9) paranoia;   (10) agoraphobia

III: (1) nostalgia; (2) benevolence; (3) satiety; (4) frustration; (5) antipathy; (6) weltschmerz; (7) misogyny; (8) compunction; (9) vindictiveness; (10) superciliousness; (11) lethargy; (12) enervation; (13) ennui; (14) misanthropy; (15) vicariousness

IV: (1) anthropology; (2) geology; (3) archaeology; (4) embryology; (5) entomology; (6) ethnology; (7) etymology; (8) ornithology; (9) philology; (10) psychology

V: (1) S; (2) O; (3) N; (4) S; (5) S; (6) O; (7) O; (8) N; (9) O; (10) S

VI: (1) penury; (2) malinger; (3) jingoism; (4) braggadocio; (5) panacea; (6) peccadillo; (7) fiasco; (8) anomaly; (9) chicanery; (10) idiosyncrasy

VII: (1) g; (2) e; (3) c; (4) a; (5) h; (6) j; (7) i; (8) d; (9) f; (10) b

VIII: (1) a; (2) b; (3) b; (4) c; (5) c

IX: (1) c; (2) a; (3) b; (4) a; (5) b

X: (1) large; (2) one; (3) mind or spirit; (4) well; (5) wish; (6) say; (7) make; (8) marriage; (9) God; (10) two, twice

Scoring: one point for each
correct answer
Maximum score: 95
              Your Score: ....
80–95   Excellent
70–79   Good
51–69   Passing
 0–50   Poor

If your score isn't as creditable as you would like, don't feel the least bit discouraged. And whatever your age, don't use the excuse that "you can't teach an old dog new tricks."

This ancient belief has been entirely disproved by an exhaustive series of tests conducted under the direction of Dr. Irving Lorge, brilliant young psychologist of Columbia University. He established the fact that the human mind retains its full powers up to the most advanced age. The *speed* of thinking is usually a little less, but *without exception,* the power element shows no decline whatsoever with people even up to ninety years of age.

So Dr. Lorge has deprived us of the easy and comfortable alibi of age!

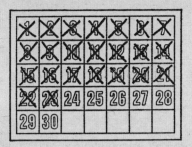

Can You Meet
This Challenge?

Continuing the inductive, psychological, and indirect method of building vocabulary that we discussed in Chapter XX, we shall now throw you pell-mell into a quiz to test your understanding of a group of words before going on to consider them. In each of the fifteen sentences that follow you will find one or two words in italics. If the words are strange to you, read the sentence carefully. Then, in each case, put a check after the particular phrase—*a, b,* or *c*—that you think comes nearest the meaning.

I

1. If spelling is your *bête noire,*
    a. You love spelling.
    b. You are a good speller.
    c. You hate spelling.
2. If your friend looked *cadaverous,* you would say to him:

    a. When did you get up from sleep?
    b. Better stop eating so many sweets.
    c. What cemetery do you live in?

3. If the President wants *carte blanche* in allocating defense funds,
    a. He wishes no strings to be attached to the money.
    b. He does not want special funds earmarked.
    c. He wants instructions from Congress on how to spend.

4. *Esoteric* knowledge is
    a. Knowledge possessed by a few.
    b. Useless knowledge.
    c. Knowledge that was buried with the fall of ancient civilization.

5. The man who says that psychology is his *forte* means
    a. He hates the subject.
    b. He's particularly good in the subject.
    c. He loves the subject.

6. When you come to an *impasse,*
    a. Stop, look, and listen!
    b. You find yourself completely blocked in a certain situation.
    c. Wait for a guide to show you the way out.

7. *Incongruous* means
    a. Out of place or character.
    b. Not honest.
    c. Not useful.

8. *Docile* people are
    a. Stupid.
    b. Lovable.
    c. Easily managed.

9. *Miscegenation* is marriage between
    a. A Presbyterian and an Episcopalian.
    b. An heiress and a pauper.
    c. People of different races.

10. *Moribund* institutions
    a. Are passing out of existence.

    b. Are in charge of dishonest people.

    c. Are undemocratic.

11. A *nebulous* idea is one that is

    a. Heaven-sent.

    b. Vague.

    c. As pure as clouds.

12. People who indulge in *recriminations* are probably

    a. Playing a game.

    b. Quarreling.

    c. Writing letters.

13. The *repercussions* of an event must happen

    a. Before.

    b. After.

    c. At the same time.

14. *Scurrilous* language would more than likely be heard in

    a. The halls of Congress.

    b. A quarrel between two stevedores.

    c. A sermon.

15. *Soporific* speakers tend to

    a. Stimulate you to action.

    b. Appeal to your nobler instincts.

    c. Put you to sleep.

ANSWERS: (1) c;   (2) c;   (3) a;   (4) a;   (5) b;
         (6) b;   (7) a;   (8) c;   (9) c;   (10) a;
         (11) b;   (12) b;   (13) b;   (14) b;   (15) c

II

Now pronounce the words—several times. Hear them in your own voice and you begin to feel more and more at home with them!

1. *bête noire* (bet-NWAHR')
2. *cadaverous* (kə-DAV'-ə-rəs)
3. *carte blanche* (kart-BLAHNSH')
4. *esoteric* (es'-ə-TAIR'-ik)

5. *forte* (FORT′)
6. *impasse* (IM′-pass)
7. *incongruous* (in-KONG′-grōo-əs)
      noun, *incongruity:* (in′-kəng-GRŌO′-ə-tee)
8. *docile* (DOSS′-əl)
      noun, *docility:* (doss-SIL′-ə-tee)
9. *miscegenation* (miss′-ə-jə-NAY′-shən)
10. *moribund* (MAWR′-ə-bund′ or MAHR′-ə-bund′)
11. *nebulous* (NEB′-yə-ləs)
12. *recrimination* (rə-krim′-ə-NAY′-shən)
13. *repercussion* (rep′-ər-KUSH′-ən)
14. *scurrilous* (SKUR′-ə-ləs)
15. *soporific* (sop′-ə-RIF′-ik)

III

You've mulled the words and their meanings over in your mind. You've said them aloud. Now write them, one to each definition. (Some of the words may be required more than once.)

1. A particular object of hate or dread   B ....
2. Pale; ghastly   C ....
3. Unconditional permission or author-
   ity   C ....
4. Confined to a select circle   E ....
5. One's strong point   F ....
6. Corpselike   C ....
7. A blind alley; an insurmountable
   obstacle   I ....
8. For the initiated few   E ....
9. Inadaptable; out of place   I ....
10. Tractable   D ....
11. Dead end   I ....
12. An object of dread   B ....
13. Marriage of mixed races   M ....
14. In a dying state   M ....
15. Hazy; indistinct   N ....
16. Charges retorted; abusive argument   R ....

17. Reverberations   R ....
18. Grossly offensive or vulgar   S ....
19. Tending to produce sleep   S ....
20. Pale and gaunt   C ....

ANSWERS: (1) bête noire; (2) cadaverous; (3) carte
         blanche; (4) esoteric; (5) forte; (6) ca-
         daverous; (7) impasse; (8) esoteric; (9)
         incongruous; (10) docile; (11) impasse;
         (12) bête noire; (13) miscegenation; (14)
         moribund; (15) nebulous; (16) recrimina-
         tions; (17) repercussions; (18) scurrilous;
         (19) soporific; (20) cadaverous

IV

Here is another list of twenty descriptive phrases. We
have shuffled the words, and again have repeated several.
Follow the same procedure as in Section III.

1. Intermarriage of races   M ....
2. Confined to a particular circle   E ....
3. Permission without condition   C ....
4. Inextricable difficulty   I ....
5. Incompatible   I ....
6. On the point of dying   M ....
7. Confused and hazy   N ....
8. Vulgarly abusive   S ....
9. Black marries white   M ....
10. Dead end   I ....
11. Ghastly   C ....
12. Bugaboo   B ....
13. Something in which one excels   F ....
14. Manageable   D ....
15. Hazy   N ....
16. Echoes   R ....
17. Producing sleep   S ....
18. Occidental weds Oriental   M ....
19. For a few   E ....
20. Specialty   F ....

ANSWERS: (1) miscegenation; (2) esoteric; (3) carte blanche; (4) impasse; (5) incongruous; (6) moribund; (7) nebulous; (8) scurrilous; (9) miscegenation; (10) impasse; (11) cadaverous; (12) bête noire; (13) forte; (14) docile; (15) nebulous; (16) repercussions; (17) soporific; (18) miscegenation; (19) esoteric; (20) forte

V

Let's try something new now, putting you more on your own. Write the word that best completes each sentence.

1. Some people think that fidelity in marriage is ....

2. Knowledge of Oriental magic is highly ....

3. If you hate cats with a purple passion, then cats are your ....

4. A man suffering from consumption may look ....

5. The facts behind a politician's statements are often ....

6. What is the one thing you hate or fear most? What is your particular ....?

7. After a dynamic Presidential speech one often hears .... abroad.

8. Marriage between people of different races is called ....

9. When a husband and wife quarrel they frequently indulge in bitter ....

10. A lecturer with a monotonous voice often produces a .... effect.

11. Angry truckdrivers frequently use .... language.

12. What are you most skilled at? What is your special ....?

13. The cow is a very .... animal.

14. A fat and awkward girl would look .... in the ballet.
15. She gave her husband .... to invite any-one he wanted to the party.

ANSWERS: (1) moribund; (2) esoteric; (3) bête noire; (4) cadaverous; (5) nebulous; (6) bête noire; (7) repercussions; (8) miscegena-tion; (9) recriminations; (10) soporific; (11) scurrilous; (12) forte; (13) docile; (14) incongruous; (15) carte blanche

VI

Your tasks are becoming more challenging with each new exercise—and here is a particularly hard one. Write the word that is *opposite* in meaning to each of the following phrases. *Note well: Opposite, not synonymous!* Again, some will be required more than once.

1. Known to all   ....
2. Caucasian marries Caucasian   ....
3. In keeping with surroundings   ....
4. Stimulating, like coffee   ....
5. Radiantly healthy   ....
6. Limited power   ....
7. Crystal clear   ....
8. Easy sailing   ....
9. One's weak suit   ....
10. Restricted power   ....
11. Mutual praise   ....
12. The thing you love most   ....
13. Decent in expression   ....
14. Something in which one is unskilled ....
15. In a healthy state   ....
16. Stubborn   ....
17. Not the least bit hazy   ....
18. Esoteric   ....

19. Keeps you awake ....
20. Marriage of white to white ....

ANSWERS: (1) esoteric; (2) miscegenation; (3) incongruous; (4) soporific; (5) cadaverous; (6) carte blanche; (7) nebulous; (8) impasse; (9) forte; (10) carte blanche; (11) recriminations; (12) bête noire; (13) scurrilous; (14) forte; (15) moribund; (16) docile; (17) nebulous; (18) esoteric; (19) soporific; (20) miscegenation

VII

It is extraordinarily difficult to write the definitions of a word. And yet your understanding of a word must be somewhat nebulous if you can't define it. Try your hand at writing brief definitions of the following words:

1. *bête noire* ....
....

2. *cadaverous* ....
....

3. *carte blanche* ....
....

4. *esoteric* ....
....

5. *forte* ....
....

6. *impasse* ....
....

7. *incongruous* ....
....

8. *docile* ....
....

9. *miscegenation* ....
....

10. *moribund* ....
....

11. *nebulous* ....

....

12. *recriminations* ....

....

13. *repercussions* ....

....

14. *scurrilous* ....

....

15. *soporific* ....

....

ANSWERS: 1. A person or object of fear or aversion; a bugbear
2. Pale, ghastly, corpselike
3. An order signed in blank; unconditional authority
4. Adapted exclusively for the initiated and enlightened few
5. Your strong point; that skill in which you excel
6. An impassable road or way; a blind alley; an insurmountable situation
7. Out of place; inharmonious
8. Easily led and managed
9. Marriage between people of two different races; mixed marriage
10. In a dying state
11. Hazy; cloudy; amorphous
12. Accusations repelled by other accusations; abusive arguments
13. Reverberations; echoes
14. Coarse, opprobrious abuse
15. Tending to cause or to produce sleep

You have learned the words in this chapter in the way that you normally learn words in your everyday life. That is, you first come across a new word in a book or in your newspaper, or you hear someone speak it. You wonder at its meaning. Your understanding of the word gradually clears, and each time you see or hear it again, you find that your knowledge of it is becoming more secure. Finally you learn to know it so well that you dare to use it in your writing and speaking. You might even be able to define it, as you have done in this chapter, if you were called upon to do so, although this is the hardest challenge of all. That is, the methods we are using in this book are the methods by which you naturally and unself-consciously learned most of the words in your vocabulary before you picked up and started working with us.

Words That Describe You

Keep in mind this important point in reference to your vocabulary improvement program. If you can personalize your new words, if you can make them bear some relationship to yourself and your way of living, you then materially increase your chances of making these words a *permanent* part of your vocabulary.

You cannot learn words in a vacuum. That is, if a word cannot be made to have a bearing on your life, if it cannot be brought within the circle of your own thoughts, if it cannot be made a part of your own personality or of your attitudes, then that word will remain useless to you.

I

The words in this chapter should, therefore, be thought of in reference to *yourself*. Let us, for the next few pages, consider your own attitudes toward life.

1. Do you view with a certain degree of tolerance the

eccentricities and foibles of other humans? Are you broad-minded, sympathetic, inclined to see the other person's point of view? Do your tastes cover a wide range? For example, in your reading, can you be interested in everything from detective stories to Russian novels? In your eating, do your likes run the gamut from a New England dinner of boiled beef to a gourmet's delight of exotic seafood? Yes? Then we will characterize you as a person whose tastes, interests, desires, and sympathies are, in one word, *catholic*.

2. Do you make trouble by your unreasoning, irascible, and vainglorious patriotism? Do you carry your jealousy of your country's honor to an absurd and ridiculous extreme? You are *chauvinistic*.

3. Are you inclined to give up the struggle before the battle is lost? Are you all too ready to lay down your arms and admit defeat at a time when braver and more optimistic souls would see many reasons for carrying on? You are a *defeatist*.

4. Do you like to dabble in the arts or the sciences? Fool a little bit with photography, only to abandon it, say, for stamp collecting? If you flit like a butterfly from interest to interest, never concentrating for any length of time on one, you are a *dilettante*.

5. Are you one whose main purpose in life seems to be the attainment of pleasure? Do you put too high a value on the luxuries of life? Are you fond of eating and drinking, and are you an expert in the choice of wines and foods? You are an *epicurean*.

6. Perhaps you find yourself in such a financial position that you must calculate closely the money costs of all your activities. Then, of course, you must practice economy. But are you *too* close-fisted with money? Do people call you stingy? You are *parsimonious*.

7. Do you look with contempt upon artists and those with an artistic temperament? Are you ignorant? Prejudiced? Blindly conventional? Narrow-minded? Do you tend to have low aims in life and are you inclined to be materialistic? You are a *philistine*.

8. Are you wasteful, extravagant, inclined to spend your money, time, energy, and talent without care or thought? You are a *profligate*.

9. Do you meet the tragedies of life with a stiff upper lip? Do you conceal your emotions, no matter how great your mental or physical suffering may be? You are a *stoic*.

10. Finally, do you happen to know a man who is so absurdly and slavishly devoted to his wife that he is the joke of the neighborhood? He is *uxorious*.

II

Now that was a big order. Possibly many, or even all, of the words of this chapter are unfamiliar to you. If so, the exercises to come will make them your best friends. Or possibly you are well acquainted with most or all of them. In that case, the pages that follow will provide an opportunity for an even warmer and deeper intimacy.

First, of course, we pronounce them aloud—several times. As you say each one, think of, or check back on, the meaning, and decide whether the adjective or noun does, or does not, fit you, personally; then check the proper box.

1. *catholic* (KATH′-ə-lik)   Yes...... No......
2. *chauvinistic* (shō-və-NIS′-tik)   Yes...... No......
3. *defeatist* (də-FEE′-tist)   Yes...... No......
4. *dilettante* (DIL′-ə-tahnt′; *also*, dil-ə-TAN′-tee)   Yes...... No......
5. *epicurean* (ep′-ə-kyə-REE′-ən)   Yes...... No......
6. *parsimonious* (pahr-sə-MŌ′-nee-əs)   Yes...... No......
7. *philistine* (FIL′-ə-steen′ *or* fə-LISS′-tin)   Yes...... No......
8. *profligate* (PROF′-lə-gət)   Yes...... No......
9. *stoic* (STŌ′-ik)   Yes...... No......
10. *uxorious* (uk-SAWR′-ee-əs)   Yes...... No......

III

To get on still better terms with these ten words, fill each one in next to its key phrase or statement. Initial letters are provided. Try not to look at Sections I or II except as a desperate last resort.

KEY		WORD
A-1.	A dabbler in art matters	D ....
2.	Unduly sparing in money	P ....
3.	Narrow-minded; uncultured	P ....
4.	Always expecting failure	D ....
5.	With liberal views and wide tastes	C ....
B-1.	Niggardly	P ....
2.	Exaggeratedly patriotic	C ....
3.	Foolishly devoted to one's wife	U ....
4.	Believes that pleasure is chief good	E ....
5.	Recklessly extravagant	P ....
C-1.	Absurdly nationalistic	C ....
2.	Materialistic	P ....
3.	"Give up the ship!"	D ....
4.	Stingy	P ....
5.	Superficial amateur	D ....
D-1.	Penny-pinching	P ....
2.	Indifference to pleasure or pain	S ....
3.	A severe ascetic	S ....
4.	Ignorant and narrow-minded	P ....
5.	Given to dissipation	P ....
E-1.	Comprehensive in sympathies	C ....
2.	Follows a branch of knowledge superficially	D ....
3.	Loves the refinements of pleasure	E ....
4.	Excessively patriotic	C ....
5.	"Eat and be merry!"	E ....
F-1.	With exquisite taste in food and drink	E ....
2.	Abandoned in character and principles	P ....
3.	Insensible to virtue and decency	P ....

4. Wasteful of money   P ....
5. Excessively fond of one's wife   U ....

ANSWERS: A. (1) dilettante;   (2) parsimonious;   (3)
          philistine;   (4) defeatist;   (5) catholic
          B. (1) parsimonious;   (2) chauvinistic;   (3)
          uxorious;   (4) epicurean;   (5) profligate
          C. (1) chauvinistic;   (2) philistine;   (3)
          defeatist;   (4) parsimonious;   (5) dilettante
          D. (1) parsimonious;   (2) stoic;   (3) stoic;
          (4) philistine;   (5) profligate
          E. (1) catholic;   (2) dilettante;   (3) epicu-
          rean;   (4) chauvinistic;   (5) epicurean
          F. (1) epicurean;   (2) profligate;   (3) prof-
          ligate;   (4) profligate;   (5) uxorious

IV

Each of the nine paragraphs that follow describes one
of the words that we have been talking about. Can you
tell which one and write it in?

1. My taste is highly cultivated for all things. While
   I am not by any means promiscuous in my interests, still I can always see the other person's point of
   view. I am tolerant to a great degree, for my sympathies are comprehensive and all embracing. I am
   ....

2. Frugal? To the last ditch! People have even accused
   me of being tight-fisted and stingy, and I am afraid
   that if they are referring to my attitude toward
   spending money, they are correct. I am ....

3. I have been accused of being without emotions, but
   the fact is that I have merely trained myself to be
   indifferent alike to pain and pleasure. I am a (an)
   ....

4. I am greatly interested in the fine arts, but being a
   person of independent means I don't have to really
   work hard at them, and it isn't necessary for me to

make a living out of them. They are more or less of a pastime with me. I am a (an) ....

5. My country? The best, the finest, the truest, the richest, the bravest, and if you don't think so you had better keep away from me. Why, I can scarcely find adjectives to describe my pride in my birthplace or to show the utter contempt I feel for all other lands. I am ....

6. I don't think it's fair to call me a traitor to my ideals. It's just that I do not care to fight what I know to be a losing battle. I am a (an) ....

7. Other people can waste time pampering artists and poets if they want to, but give me a he-man every time—the kind who is interested in material things like making money. And while we're on the subject, those people who keep their noses buried in books all the time and who are always worrying about knowledge and progress and liberalism! Well, I can put them also on my list of people who won't be missed! I am a (an) ....

8. Laugh at me if you like and say that my wife uses me as a footstool. I don't care! Nothing I do will ever be good enough for her! I am ....

9. As for me, I like my pleasure. Other people can work and slave and worry about the future and save their money, but not I! Give me a good time any day! Let the little milquetoasts keep their noses to the grindstone and lead temperate lives. I figure money is made to spend, and I believe in the old proverb, "Eat, drink, and be merry." I am a (an) ....

ANSWERS: (1) catholic; (2) parsimonious; (3) stoic; (4) dilettante; (5) chauvinistic; (6) defeatist; (7) philistine; (8) uxorious; (9) epicurean

V

By now you are developing real and assured control over these words. Therefore, you will be able to sail through the next exercise with the greatest of ease and a perfect or near-perfect score. Check *a, b,* or *c.*

1. A person of *catholic* tastes is
   a. religious.
   b. moral.
   c. sympathetic.

2. If you met an American *chauvinist* it would be safe to remark:
   a. "I would really rather live abroad."
   b. "I love my country and I despise all other nations."
   c. "Listen, America has plenty of black marks on her record! How about the Spanish-American war?"

3. The *defeatist* is a
   a. coward.
   b. pessimist.
   c. bully.

4. Anybody knows that a *dilettante* is
   a. a master of the arts.
   b. a struggling young artist.
   c. one who follows the arts as a pastime.

5. The *epicurean*'s greatest delight comes from
   a. pleasure.
   b. cruelty.
   c. self-torment.

6. *Parsimonious?* He's a
   a. miser.
   b. spendthrift.
   c. philanthropist.

7. While the word *philistine* is of Biblical origin, it now merely refers to a person who is
   a. hypocritically pious.

      b. narrow-minded; opposed to progress and learning.

      c. wealthy and hardhearted.

8. Few people realize that a *stoic* doesn't mind

      a. pleasure and pain.

      b. spending money.

      c. getting drunk.

9. An *uxorious* man

      a. foolishly and fondly dotes on his wife.

      b. is completely penniless.

      c. always complains of the way life treats him.

10. A *profligate* person is

      a. dishonest.

      b. insincere.

      c. wasteful.

ANSWERS: (1) c;   (2) b;   (3) b;   (4) c;   (5) a;
            (6) a;   (7) b;   (8) a;   (9) a;   (10) c

VI

And now for the acid test of your learning. Without checking back to any previous material, can you write each word next to its definition?

1. Broad-minded in views   ....

2. An exaggerated patriot   ....

3. Follows the policy or practice of admitting defeat too quickly   ....

4. One who dabbles in art and letters   ....

5. One who makes a profession of pleasure. A connoisseur of food and wine ....

6. Unnecessarily frugal   ....

7. A person with a plebeian type of mind. An individual of materialistic tastes who is interested neither in art nor letters   ....

8. Completely given up to dissipation; dissolute; wasteful   ....

9. A person showing no emotion over
   pleasure or pain   ....

10. Extravagantly submissive to, and doting
    upon, one's wife   ....

ANSWERS: (1) catholic; (2) chauvinist; (3) defeatist;
          (4) dilettante; (5) epicurean; (6) parsimo-
          nious; (7) philistine; (8) profligate; (9)
          stoic; (10) uxorious

In all likelihood this has not been an easy chapter. But it
is true, isn't it, that all learning and all the skills are ac-
quired only by dogged, systematic, and intensive work?
After all, the greatest obstacle to anyone's getting ahead
is just plain laziness. The average man makes a fair success with very ordinary effort, and conversely, most people
lose out in life just because they won't take the trouble to
win. That's why there's always so much room at the top.

If you will make use of the ideas in this book, they will
open many doors to you. If you will make the precepts of
this book a lifetime habit, the habit will take care of you,
and lead you to greater success. Success itself is a habit.

Life has many prizes waiting for the winner. And, after
all, it's a lot less exhausting to win than to worry.

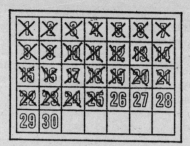

French Phrases You Can Use

The rivers of all languages have flowed into the vast reservoir of English.

The following paragraph will give you just a hint of its varied sources. Each of the italicized words came into English from a foreign language.

"The *sky* was teeming rain. The *boss* has a touch of *influenza*. He came up on the *veranda*, put down his *mammoth umbrella*, entered the comfortable *oasis* of his living room, and sat down. He filled his pipe with *tobacco*, warmed himself first with hot *cocoa*, then *coffee*, and listened to his pet *canary* sing."

Here are the parentages of these words:

sky	Old Norse	oasis	Egyptian
boss	Dutch	tobacco	West Indian
influenza	Italian	cocoa	Mexican
veranda	Portuguese	coffee	Arabic
mammoth	Russian	canary	Spanish
umbrella	Italian		

The main contributors to English, however, are not the languages from which the above examples have been taken. They are, rather, French, Latin, and Greek.

French, as would be understandable, has added a large number of delicate and graceful words and phrases to our speech. Many of these have been adopted so recently that they still retain their Gallic flavor.

I

Here are ten common French importations:

1. If a prisoner of war were being tortured and were on the point of death, the final stroke that killed him would be the *coup de grâce*. Any blow that puts a suffering and greatly weakened animal, person, or institution out of its misery is a *coup de grâce*. Thus, we will say, a conqueror has allowed a subject nation to continue, for a time, with nominal independence. When and if that conqueror decides to overrun the vanquished nation and completely destroy its last vestige of freedom, he will be delivering the *coup de grâce*.

2. Anyone who is in the way, out of place, or not wanted is *de trop*. If little brother insists on sitting in the living room when his sister's beau comes a-calling he is considered *de trop*.

3. In a sophisticated conversation, slightly off-color or improper remarks are sometimes made in terms that seem innocent. Any word or phrase that has two meanings, one of them an indelicate one, is called a *double-entendre*.

4. You are *en rapport* with someone when there is a perfect meeting of minds and a complete absence of friction.

5. A cooperative spirit on the part of a group, combined with an enthusiastic submergence of self-interest for the sake of the common good, is called *esprit de corps*. A crack regiment is sometimes famed for its *esprit de corps*.

6. Napoleon proved himself to be a leader *par excellence*. Escoffier, noted the world over for his cuisine, was

a chef *par excellence*. Ralph Waldo Emerson, we might say, was the interpreter of Plato *par excellence*.

7. If your mind is perfectly attuned to your surroundings, if you are alive and alert to all that is going on around you, if you are on guard, wide awake, eager, expectant, you are on the *qui vive*.

8. A medley of things, an assorted and heterogeneous mixture of great variety, is called a *potpourri*.

9 and 10. Have you ever met a man or woman with perfect poise? Do you notice how he or she says exactly the correct and charming thing at the proper time? Never is such a person guilty of a *faux pas,* an embarrassing mistake; on the contrary, your perfectly poised, sophisticated, cosmopolitan friend is the possessor of *savoir-faire*.

II

The pronunciation of words from the French does not require a Gallic accent—all have been somewhat Anglicized. When you use such a word, and we expect that you occasionally will, don't pause significantly as if you were about to break into song. On the contrary, say the Parisian import as naturally as any other word—after all, thousands upon thousands of English words come from foreign tongues: from Greek, Latin, Old Norse, German, Dutch, Italian, Portuguese, Chinese, Japanese, etc.

True, with French imports, Anglicization has not gone quite as far as with most others, so do not be surprised that the sounds you will be making will not account for all the letters in every word.

Here, then, is a close approximation of our terms from the French. Practice them carefully, aloud, and many times.

1. *coup de grâce* (ko͞o′-də-GRAHSS′)
2. *de trop* (də-TRŌ)
3. *double-entendre* (DO͞O′-blə-ahn-TAHN′-drə)
4. *en rapport* (ahn′-ra′-PAWR′)

5. *esprit de corps* (es-pree'-də-KAWR')
6. *par excellence* (pahr'-ek-sə-LAHNSS')
7. *qui vive* (kee'-VEEV')
8. *potpourri* (pō'-poo'-REE')
9. *faux pas* (fō'-PAH')
10. *savoir-faire* (sav'-wahr'-FAIR')

(Incidentally, all ten phrases still maintain their foreign citizenship—therefore they are always underlined when written or italicized when printed.)

III

The literal translations of these ten French terms will help establish the meanings in your mind.

1. *Coup de grâce*	....	Blow of mercy
2. *De trop*	....	Too much
3. *Double-entendre*	....	Double meaning
4. *En rapport*	....	In harmonious relation
5. *Esprit de corps*	....	Spirit of the body
6. *Par excellence*	....	By excellence
7. *Qui vive*	....	Who lives
8. *Potpourri*	....	Rotten pot
9. *Faux pas*	....	False step
10. *Savoir-faire*	....	To know how to do

IV

The ten words of this chapter have not yet been defined for you. Their meanings have at most been sketched in. Nevertheless a careful rereading of Section I will make it possible for you to write the correct French terms next to each of the following synonyms or synonymous phrases. Some of the terms will be called for many times in the lists that are given below.

A 1. Out of place   D ....
   2. Group enthusiasm   E ....

3. Double meaning   D ....

4. Surpassingly good   P ....

5. On the alert   *on the* Q ....

B 1. In the very choicest manner   P ....

  2. In agreement   E ....

  3. In the way   D ....

  4. Mixture   P ....

  5. Decisive blow   C ....

C 1. On your toes   *on the* Q ....

  2. Two's company   D ....

  3. Finishing stroke   C ....

  4. Preeminently   P ....

  5. Off-color ambiguity   D ....

D 1. In harmonious relationship   E ....

  2. On guard   *on the* Q ....

  3. Jealous regard for the honor of the group   E ....

  4. Medley   P ....

  5. Embarrassing error   F ....

E 1. Poise   S ....

  2. Little of everything   P ....

  3. In accord   E ....

  4. Knowing and doing the graceful thing   S ....

  5. Embarrassing mistake   F ....

ANSWERS: A. (1) *de trop;* (2) *esprit de corps;* (3) *double-entendre;* (4) *par excellence;* (5) *on the qui vive*

B. (1) *par excellence;* (2) *en rapport;* (3) *de trop;* (4) *potpourri;* (5) *coup de grâce*

C. (1) *on the qui vive;* (2) *de trop;* (3) *coup de grâce;* (4) *par excellence;* (5) *double-entendre*

D. (1) *en rapport;* (2) *on the qui vive;* (3) *esprit de corps;* (4) *potpourri;* (5) *faux pas*

E. (1) *savoir-faire;* (2) *potpourri;* (3) *en rapport;* (4) *savoir-faire;* (5) *faux pas*

V

Below you will find ten statements in which the French words and phrases we have been studying are used; some are true, others false. Write T or F next to each statement.

1. The divorce was granted to the wife, who also got custody of the children and the dog, and possession of the home, furniture, bank accounts, and both cars. On top of all this, as the *coup de grâce,* she was awarded 75 per cent of her husband's salary as alimony.   ....

2. Someone we enjoy being with is usually *de trop.*   ....

3. Naïve girls indulge in frequent *doubles-entendres.*   ....

4. A husband and wife should be *en rapport.*   ....

5. A defeated army is full of *esprit de corps.*   ....

6. Sarah Bernhardt was admitted to be an actress *par excellence.*   ....

7. A book of famous quotations is a *pot-pourri* of literary gems.   ....

8. A prize-fighter must be on the *qui vive* when he is in the ring.   ....

9. A finishing school claims to give young girls *savoir-faire.*   ....

10. A *faux pas* is generally embarrassing.   ....

ANSWERS: (1) T;   (2) F;   (3) F;   (4) T;   (5) F;
         (6) T;   (7) T;   (8) T;   (9) T;   (10) T

VI

Here, finally, is the last test of your familiarity with the French imports studied in this chapter. Without reference to previous material, fill in each term next to its definition. Can you spell them correctly?

1. The mortal stroke ....
2. Said of a person who is in the way, out of place, or not wanted ....
3. A word or phrase with double meaning ....
4. In harmonious relation one with the other ....
5. The common devotion of members to an organization ....
6. Preeminent; beyond comparison ....
7. A mixture; a medley; a mélange ....
8. The challenge of a French sentinel, meaning "Who goes there?" Hence, on the alert ....
9. The ability to say and do the right thing at the right time ....
10. A misstep; an embarrassing mistake ....

ANSWERS: (1) *coup de grâce;* (2) *de trop;* (3) *double-entendre;* (4) *en rapport;* (5) *esprit de corps;* (6) *par excellence;* (7) *potpourri;* (8) *qui vive;* (9) *savoir-faire;* (10) *faux pas*

These ten phrases are only a few of the thousands of French imports that have become the adopted children of our language. Used with discretion, they can take their places as the grace notes of cultured conversation and writing. You will be surprised how many you will hear and see if you start listening and watching for them.

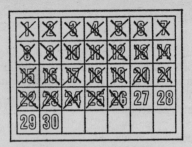

Words About Words

Every specialty, naturally, has its own terminology. The lawyers, the preachers, the doctors, all speak their own language. The physician, for instance, has to know the names of 707 different arteries, 71 bones, 79 convolutions, 433 muscles, 230 nerves, 403 veins, 295 poisons, 109 tumors, and also about 10,000 drugs.

The philologist speaks his own language, too, and unless we were versed in his speech we would find it difficult to understand him when he talked of phonology, phonemics, and morphology.

We can, however, pick a few of the more popular words that lie in this field of language, ones that we can use in common conversation. For some of the most interesting words in our language are words about words. Here are ten such:

1. *anticlimax* (an'-tee-KLY'-max')
2. *analogy* (a-NAL'-ə-jee)
3. *ambiguity* (am'-bə-GYOO'-ə-tee)

4. *cliché* (klee-SHAY′)
5. *epigram* (EP′-ə-gram′)
6. *euphemism* (YŌŌ′-fə-miz′-əm)
7. *redundancy* (ree-DUN′-dən-see)
8. *non sequitur* (non-SEK′-wə-tər)
9. *persiflage* (PUR′-sə-flahzh′)
10. *simile* (SIM′-ə-lee)

I

Here is an example of each:

1. *Anticlimax*
   Dr. Jones and Dr. Smith will be guest speakers at the County Medical Society meeting Tuesday night at Mineola. Dr. Jones will take his topic from the psalm: "Behold how good and pleasant it is for brethren to dwell together in unity." Dr. Smith will speak on flat feet.

2. *Analogy*
   Your body is like a machine. Put in the proper fuel and it will function efficiently.

3. *Ambiguity*
   The farmer's helper took his car out of the garage. (Whose car did he take?)

4. *Cliché*
   "It's a great life if you don't weaken."

5. *Epigram*
   It is more blessed to give than to receive.

6. *Euphemism*
   "Mortician" or "funeral director" for *undertaker*. "Lady of the night" for *prostitute*. "Powder room" for *toilet*. "Pass away" for *die*. "Limb" for *leg*. "Derrière" or "rear" for *behind*. "Intimate relations" for *sexual intercourse*.

7. *Redundancy*
   The biggest, the greatest, the most stupendous show on earth.

8. *Non Sequitur*
   "Despite her age, her interest in music never flagged.
   During the past year she has crocheted a bedspread
   and a tablecloth."

9. *Persiflage*
   "Man never knows precisely what is right
   So, torn between a purpose and a doubt,
   He first makes windows to let in the light,
   And then hangs curtains up to shut it out."

10. *Simile*
    As thick as seagulls on a rock.

II

We have spoken before of noun endings (*-ity, -ence,
-ance, -ion,* etc.), and have changed adjectives into nouns.
Now, in reverse, let us change nouns into adjectives.

Some common adjective endings are *-ic* (as in *dynam-
ic*), *-ical* (as in *biological*), *-ous* (as in *marvelous*), *-ant*
and *-ent* (as in *triumphant, persistent*), *-al* (as in *banal*),
and *-ive* (as in *active*).

Use your innate sense of language to change the following nouns into their adjective forms. Note also the examples of other noun-adjective transformations presented
as guides, and test the sound of the form you devise in the
sentence offered.

1. Change *anticlimax* to an adjective.
   (Similar transformation: *climax—climactic*)
      After the great naval victory, the sinking of a
      single enemy trawler was ....

2. Change *analogy* to an adjective.
   (*bigamy—bigamous*)
      Let us discuss an .... situation.

3. Change *ambiguity* to an adjective.
   (*superfluity—superfluous*)
      That is an .... statement.

4. Change *epigram* to an adjective.
   (*diagram—diagrammatic*)
      Oscar Wilde has an .... style.
5. Change *euphemism* to an adjective.
   (*antagonism—antagonistic*)
      Let us use a more .... term.
6. Change *redundancy* to an adjective.
   (*militancy—militant*)
      Your statement is ....

ANSWERS: (1) anticlimactic (an'-tee-kly-MAK'-tik); (2) analogous (a-NAL'-ə-gəs); (3) ambiguous (am-BIG'-yo͞o-əs); (4) epigrammatic (ep'-ə-grə-MAT'-ik); (5) euphemistic (yo͞o'-fə-MISS'-tik); (6) redundant (ree-DUN'-dənt)

III

Can you write the proper term next to each definition? Initial letters are provided to insure your success.

1. A rhetorical figure expressing comparison or likeness   S ....
2. Partial agreement or resemblance between things somewhat different; similarity in certain aspects   A ....
3. A light, flippant style of conversation or writing; banter; raillery   P ....
4. A stale, worn-out or stereotyped phrase, either written or spoken   C ....
5. An inference, or conclusion, that does not follow from the facts as stated   N ....
6. A gradual or sudden decrease in the importance or impressiveness of what is said; the opposite of climax; a ludicrous or ridiculous drop in thought and expression, sometimes from the sublime to the ridiculous   A ....

7. Vagueness; indefiniteness; uncertainty; an expression whose meaning can be taken in two or more ways   A ....

8. A pithy saying in prose or verse that crystallizes a wise or witty thought   E ....

9. A pleasing expression used in place of one which is plainer or more accurate but which might be offensive, embarrassing, or in bad taste   E ....

10. Unnecessary repetition or the employment of more words than are necessary   R ....

ANSWERS: (1) simile;   (2) analogy;   (3) persiflage; (4) cliché;   (5) non sequitur;   (6) anticlimax;   (7) ambiguity;   (8) epigram;   (9) euphemism;   (10) redundancy

IV

If we trace the ancestry of words, we can often throw a new light on their meanings; also, we dramatize them and make them vivid. Here are the sources, all but one of them Latin or Greek, of the ten "words about words."

1. *Anticlimax.* Greek *anti,* "opposite to," and *klimax,* "ladder." So an *anticlimax* is really the opposite of climbing up; that is, it is climbing *down* the ladder of importance.

2. *Analogy.* Greek *ana,* "according to," plus *logos,* which we have met before with the meaning of "word" or "study." In this context, *logos* means "proportion." Things *analogous* to each other, while different, are similar in proportion.

3. *Ambiguity.* Latin *ambi,* "around," plus *agere,* "to go." When you make an *ambiguous* statement you are going around the subject!

4. *Cliché.* A French word that means "an electrotype or stereotype plate for printing." This is why a

statement of yours that is stereotyped, fixed, and lacking in originality is called a *cliché*.

5. *Epigram.* Greek *epi,* "on," and *graphein,* "write."

6. *Euphemism.* Greek *eu,* "well," and *phemi,* "speak." So if you utter a *euphemism,* you are at least making an effort to give a nice turn to a subject that would otherwise be disagreeable.

7. *Redundancy.* From the Latin *red,* "back," and *unda,* "wave." The waves are driven back on the shore and repeat themselves like your words when you are redundant.

8. *Non sequitur.* The direct translation from the Latin literally means "it does not follow."

9. *Persiflage.* From the Latin *per,* meaning "through," and *sibilare,* "to hiss" or "to whistle." Possibly, since *persiflage* sometimes means banter, there may be a significance in the fact that whistling or hissing can be sounds of derision.

10. *Simile.* From the Latin *similis,* "similar."

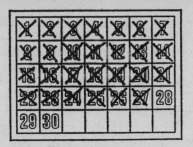

Word Building by the "Unfolding Process"

Let us now approach the problem of word development from a slightly different direction. We will still rely on the indirect method: that is, the method that shows you a word first in its context, rather than flashing it on you alone and away from its meaning in a sentence.

The meanings and uses of the following group of difficult words will be revealed by what we might call, for want of a better name, the "unfolding process." As you meet each word, even though it is for the first time, its meaning will be partially shown to you by the context, and its full meaning will gradually unfold before the chapter is over.

I

Read each sentence, noting particularly the italicized word and attempting some judgment of its meaning.

1. He lives a severe and *abstemious* life.
2. That is a *chimerical* and wholly unfounded fear.
3. Hunger among millions is a strange *facet* of affluent America.
4. Honesty is a *fetish* with him.
5. The *Machiavellian* moves of the crime syndicate are astounding.
6. *Ochlocracy* is sometimes a result of war.
7. Only God is truly *omniscient*.
8. When John's treachery was discovered, he truly became a *pariah*.
9. The dishonest employee received a *peremptory* dismissal.
10. The prisoner painted a *poignant* picture of his suffering.
11. The wife of Socrates was sour and *querulous*.
12. That is the most ridiculous and *specious* argument I have ever heard.
13. Fear of riots and civil disorders was *ubiquitous* in the late 1960s.
14. He is so *unctuous* I cannot bear him.
15. That *vainglorious* and pompous senator annoys all who know him.

II

Now pronounce the words—aloud.

1. *abstemious* (ab-STEE′-mee-əs)
2. *chimerical* (kə-MAIR′-ə-kəl)
3. *facet* (FASS′-ət)
4. *fetish* (FET′-ish *or* FEE′-tish)
5. *Machiavellian* (mak′-ee-ə-VEL′-ee-ən)
6. *ochlocracy* (ok-LOK′-rə-see)
7. *omniscient* (om-NISH′-ənt)
8. *pariah* (pə-RY′-ə)
9. *peremptory* (pə-REMP′-tə-ree)
10. *poignant* (POIN′-yənt *or* POIN′-ənt)
11. *querulous* (KWAIR′-ə-ləs)

12. *specious* (SPEE'-shəs)
13. *ubiquitous* (yōō-BIK'-wə-təs)
14. *unctuous* (UNK'-chōō-əs)
15. *vainglorious* (vain-GLAW'-ree-əs)

III

Feel free to refer to the sentences in Section I as you check what you think is the correct synonym or synonymous phrase for each word.

1. *abstemious*
   a. licentious
   b. miserly
   c. sparing in the use of food and drink
2. *chimerical*
   a. foolish
   b. fanciful
   c. difficult
3. *facet*
   a. side; aspect
   b. tap
   c. failure
4. *fetish*
   a. shoe
   b. object of worship
   c. love
5. *Machiavellian*
   a. kingly
   b. politically cunning
   c. angelic
6. *ochlocracy*
   a. dictatorship
   b. mob rule
   c. democracy
7. *omniscient*
   a. omnipotent
   b. rare
   c. all-knowing

8. *pariah*
   a. outcast
   b. madman
   c. expatriate

9. *peremptory*
   a. tardy
   b. fearful
   c. decisive and final

10. *poignant*
    a. piquant
    b. painfully moving
    c. bitter

11. *querulous*
    a. questioning
    b. complaining; fretful
    c. angry

12. *specious*
    a. remarkable
    b. cunning
    c. subtly false

13. *ubiquitous*
    a. ecstatic
    b. found, or existing, everywhere
    c. pestiferous

14. *unctuous*
    a. dirty
    b. unconcerned
    c. bland and smugly smooth in pretense of concern, sincerity, or spirituality

15. *vainglorious*
    a. silly
    b. boastful
    c. fastidious

ANSWERS: (1) c;   (2) b;   (3) a;   (4) b;   (5) b;
(6) b;   (7) c;   (8) a;   (9) c;   (10) b;
(11) b;   (12) c;   (13) b;   (14) c;   (15) b

IV

Gradually, as these words "unfold" for you, you will begin to feel more and more power over them. You met each word in context; next, you heard the word in your own voice and felt comfortable with the sound of it; then you picked a synonym out of three choices. With each exercise you gained a little more self-confidence.

The next step is to see if you can think of the word when the initial letter and a synonym or brief definition are given. This exercise checks your understanding, your power of recall, and your spelling.

1. Final, brooking no opposition or argument; hence, decisive to the point of being dictatorial   P ....
2. Mob rule   O ....
3. Outcast   P ....
4. Shrewdly cunning; politically devious   M ....
5. All-knowing   O ....
6. Object of worship   F ....
7. Sharply affecting the feelings; touching   P ....
8. Found everywhere   U ....
9. One side, face, or aspect of something   F ....
10. Complaining; whining; showing discontent   Q ....
11. Very moderate, almost austere, in one's habits of eating and drinking   A ....
12. Seemingly true, but actually false   S ....
13. Boastfully conceited and self-important   V ....
14. Absurdly fanciful or unreal   C ....
15. Smooth and ingratiating, but obviously insincere, in one's pretense of piety, spirituality, concern, or earnestness   U ....

ANSWERS: (1) peremptory; (2) ochlocracy; (3) pariah; (4) Machiavellian; (5) omniscient; (6) fetish; (7) poignant; (8) ubiquitous; (9) facet; (10) querulous; (11) abstemious; (12) specious; (13) vainglorious; (14) chimerical; (15) unctuous

V

Now, without an initial letter to guide your thinking, can you write the word that each phrase or sentence hints at?

1. Reign of terror during French Revolution ....
2. An object of worship among savages ....
3. An absurd creation of the imagination ....
4. A leper ....
5. Political maneuvers of dictators of the 1930s and 1940s ....
6. Arguments of a demagogue ....
7. The ice-cream vendor and his little truck on summer afternoons ....
8. The sadness of unrequited love ....
9. Boastfulness was a characteristic of Napoleon ....
10. A complaining wife ....
11. Women who are on a reducing diet ....
12. A diamond ....
13. God ....
14. A martinet's order to an underling ....
15. A smooth appearance of sanctity ....

ANSWERS: (1) ochlocracy; (2) fetish; (3) chimerical; (4) pariah; (5) Machiavellian; (6) specious; (7) ubiquitous; (8) poignant; (9) vainglorious; (10) querulous; (11) abstemious; (12) facet; (13) omniscient; (14) peremptory; (15) unctuous

VI

"Toujours la pratique" say the French—"Always the practice." We enlarge your opportunities for practice by offering you four groups of five sentences, each sentence to be completed by one of the fifteen words. Answers follow each group so you can check your results as you go along. Some of the words may be called for more than once.

GROUP 1

1. The speaker painted a .... picture of hunger in America.
2. You may insist that everybody hates you and avoids you, but I assure you that's a .... of your diseased imagination.
3. That teacher makes a .... of discipline.
4. He is a glib, ... person; I do not trust him.
5. Your .... schemes to win the nomination will get you nowhere; already your name is anathema to most of your constituents.

ANSWERS: (1) poignant;   (2) chimera;   (3) fetish;
         (4) unctuous;   (5) Machiavellian

GROUP 2

1. At Christmas time the .... Salvation Army lassie reminds a selfish public of people for whom the season may not be merry.
2. That is a .... argument, but possibly you may get a number of unthinking people to believe it.
3. No one can call you modest or diffident; indeed, on the contrary, you are the most .... man I know.
4. Invalids, discontented wives, rejected lovers, whiny children—all these tend to be ....
5. There are so many .... to the international situation that it is difficult to guess what the future holds.

ANSWERS: (1) ubiquitous; (2) specious; (3) vainglorious; (4) querulous; (5) facets

GROUP 3

1. No one knows what is going to happen in the world.
   Things are in such an imbroglio. One would have
   to be .... to know.
2. Poor people, through lack of money, are forced to be
   ....
3. Lynching is an excellent example of ....
4. Sometimes it is necessary for an author to know
   what is going on in the minds of his characters. This
   is called ....
5. After murdering Lincoln, John Wilkes Booth became
   a ....

ANSWERS: (1) omniscient; (2) abstemious; (3) ochlocracy; (4) omniscience; (5) pariah

GROUP 4

1. Some mothers make their commands so ....
   that they antagonize their children.
2. He is winning you over to his side with ....
   reasoning.
3. His .... machinations make him the most
   feared and the least trusted man in America.
4. In the spring the color green may be said to be almost ....
5. Some housewives make an absolute .... out
   of neatness.

ANSWERS: (1) peremptory; (2) specious; (3) Machiavellian; (4) ubiquitous; (5) fetish

VII

Now we are going to ask you to think *in reverse,* for the
more angles from which we approach these words, the
more the words will become meaningful and useful to you.

Can you figure out which of the fifteen words is *opposite in meaning* to each of the following?

1. Gluttonish ....
2. Real; in actual existence ....
3. Object of hatred ....
4. Politically direct and honest ....
5. Control over the mob so that it is without power ....
6. Completely ignorant; knowing nothing ....
7. An idol, loved by all ....
8. Indecisive; wavering ....
9. Leaving the emotions unaffected ....
10. Satisfied; uncomplaining ....
11. Authentic; true in every way ....
12. Found nowhere; completely absent ....
13. Crude and boorish ....
14. Modest ....

ANSWERS: (1) abstemious; (2) chimerical; (3) fetish; (4) Machiavellian; (5) ochlocracy; (6) omniscient; (7) pariah; (8) peremptory; (9) poignant; (10) querulous; (11) specious; (12) ubiquitous; (13) unctuous; (14) vainglorious

VIII

The defining of any word is incredibly hard. Just think, for instance, of writing a definition of "blue" in such a way that a blind man will get a clear idea of what you mean. But your very attempt to define the fifteen words we have been working with will force you to think intensively about them and will clinch their meanings for you in a way that nothing else possibly could.

When you check with the answers, you cannot expect your language to be the same as that in the definitions given; but if you find that you have covered substantially the same points, you will have proof that you have mastered the fifteen words of this chapter.

1. *abstemious:* ....
....
....

2. *chimerical:* ....
....
....

3. *facet:* ....
....
....

4. *fetish:* ....
....
....

5. *Machiavellian:* ....
....
....

6. *ochlocracy:* ....
....
....

7. *omniscient:* ....
....
....

8. *pariah:* ....
....
....

9. *peremptory:* ....
....
....

10. *poignant:* ....
....
....

11. *querulous:* ....
....
....

12. *specious:* ....
....
....

13. *ubiquitous:* ....
....
....

14. *unctuous:* ....
....
....

15. *vainglorious:* ....
....
....

ANSWERS:
1. Eating and drinking sparingly; self-denying in the indulgence of the appetites
2. Merely imaginary; fanciful; fantastic; visionary
3. One of the small surfaces cut upon a diamond or other gem. By extension, a part, aspect, or point of view
4. A material object believed to be the dwelling of a spirit that will protect the owner from harm; hence, any object of devotion or blind affection
5. Of or pertaining to the Florentine politician Niccolo Machiavelli, or to a system of political trickery
6. Mob rule
7. All-knowing, or all-wise
8. A social outcast
9. Unpleasantly positive in judgment or opinion; dogmatic; dictatorial
10. Strongly affecting the emotions; touching
11. Disposed to complain or be fretful
12. Appearing right and true; plausible
13. Seeming to be everywhere at once, omnipresent
14. Smooth and bland, but insincere, in pretense of feeling, piety, spirituality, goodness, etc.
15. Excessively proud of one's attainments, accomplishments, or performance, as shown in undue elation, boasting, or self-praise.

This chapter has contained a few long and somewhat unusual words, and this leads us to a warning that we can't repeat too often. When we speak of the value of a large vocabulary, we don't mean a vocabulary of *large* words. A large word has its place. Sometimes it will crystallize a meaning that otherwise might require a whole phrase to express. Fine. Use such a word then. It will make for brevity and clarity. It is much simpler to describe a man as a "monogamist" than to have to say that "he is the type of man who believes in marrying only one wife." But never use a long word when a short one will do. Never try for fancy phrases. Persons who do that are not being "literary." They are merely being stuffy and are attempting to parade their knowledge. Don't say, "I *reside* in my *domicile*." Say, "I *live* in my *house*." You don't *commence;* you *begin.* You don't *pass away,* or *go to your reward;* you *die.* A *conflagration* is a *fire.* And you don't *retire;* you just plain *go to bed.*

The highest art is usually the simplest in form, be it sculpture or music or architecture or painting—or language.

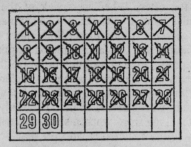

Words From
Classic Roots

We Americans are the most inventive people in the world, and we have been applying this genius continually to our language. We have been inventing words ever since the Pilgrims drew lots for land and began identifying a piece of ground as a "lot."

We have not only invented words, but, as has been indicated in this book, we have hungrily adopted them from other languages and have adapted the imported and foreign words to our own uses.

In this chapter we will explore several roads that branch off from the simple numbers *one, two,* and *three.* You may find that we will repeat some etymological roots that we have already had.

The Greek word *monos,* "one," appears in English words as *mono* or *mon.* Thus a *monocle* is a glass for one eye. *Monogamy* is one marriage. A *monogram* is a combination of two or more letters so arranged as to represent a single unit.

I

Can you think of some words beginning with *mono* or *mon*? The definitions should help you, but if you're stuck, check with the answers below.

1. .... A treatise on one subject
2. .... A speech uttered by one person
3. .... Mental derangement confined to one idea
4. .... An airplane with one pair of wings
5. .... Exclusive possession or control of any one thing
6. .... A word of one syllable
7. .... Belief in one god
8. .... One unvarying tone
9. .... Government in the hands of one ruler
10. .... Place in which a person lives alone (as one, by himself) under religious vows
11. .... The inhabitant of the place described in item 10
12. .... Continuing in one unvarying way or tone; hence, tiresome, dull

ANSWERS: (1) monograph; (2) monologue; (3) monomania; (4) monoplane; (5) monopoly; (6) monosyllable; (7) monotheism; (8) monotone; (9) monarchy; (10) monastery; (11) monk; (12) monotonous

If we analyze some of the words in the previous exercise, we discover a number of new roots.

1. In *monograph* we have Greek *graphein,* "to write," a root that appears in English words as *graph* or *gram*. For example:

graphic—written; hence, vivid
graphite—writing material
autograph—one's name written by oneself

chirography—handwriting

telegram—writing from a distance

2. In *monologue* we have Greek *logos* (discussed in Chapter 13), a root with a number of different meanings —"word," "study," "science," "proportion," or "discourse." We have already learned *entomology, philology, embryology, etymology.* Others are:

dialogue—discourse by two people

eulogy—good words

biology—science or study of life

trilogy—discourse in three parts

3. *Monomania* reminds us of other words containing *mania,* "derangement":

dipsomania—kleptomania—pyromania—nymphomania —megalomania

4. *Monotheism,* containing Greek *theos,* "god," brings to mind other words with this root:

polytheism—theology—theocracy—atheism

II

Bi- is a prefix from Latin *bis,* "twice" or "two." Thus, *biannual,* twice a year; *bicameral,* with two houses, as the Senate and the House of Representatives in our Congress, or the House of Lords and the House of Commons in England; *biceps,* a muscle having two heads of origin; *bicuspid,* a tooth ending in two points. Can you think of other words with the prefix *bi-*?

1. .... A vehicle with two wheels
2. .... Occurring every two years
3. .... Eyeglasses having two kinds of lenses
4. .... Second marriage while the first is still in effect
5. .... Every two months
6. .... Something used for two eyes
7. .... An animal with two feet
8. .... Something cooked twice; i.e., a cracker

9. .... Cut into two parts
10. .... A marine animal with two shells, as an oyster, clam, etc.

ANSWERS: (1) bicycle; (2) biennial; (3) bifocals;
(4) bigamy; (5) bimonthly; (6) binoculars; (7) biped; (8) biscuit; (9) bisect;
(10) bivalve

If we analyze the words in the previous exercise, we can find in them some useful roots.

1. The last part of *bicycle* is from Greek *kyklos*, "wheel" or "circle," a root found also in *cyclic, unicycle, tricycle*.

2. In *bigamy*, we have Greek *gamos*, a root we have already learned, and the ending of *monogamy, polygamy, misogamy*.

3. *Binoculars* contains Latin *oculus*, "eye," from which root we derive *monocle, oculist, ocular*.

4. In *biped* there is the Latin root *pedis*, "foot," also found in *pedestrian, pedal, quadruped, impede*, and *expedition*.

5. The second root in *bisect* is Latin *sectus*, "cut," from which we also derive *section, sect, insect, intersect, trisect*, etc.

III

Tri is a Latin or Greek prefix meaning "three." Thus, in music, a *triad* is a chord of three notes; a *triangle* is a figure of three angles; a *tricolor* is a flag of three colors. Now fill in the twelve spaces with the proper words made up of *tri:*

1. .... A vehicle of three wheels
2. .... Having three sides
3. .... Made up of, or pertaining to, three languages

4. .... A series of three literary or musical compositions
5. .... Every three months
6. .... The union of three persons, as the Father, the Son, and the Holy Ghost
7. .... Three people who sing a song
8. .... Consisting of three
9. .... Three children born simultaneously from the same mother
10. .... A three-legged stand, as for a camera

ANSWERS: (1) tricycle; (2) trilateral; (3) trilingual; (4) trilogy; (5) trimonthly; (6) trinity; (7) trio; (8) triple; (9) triplets; (10) tripod

Trilateral contains Latin *lateris*, "side," found also in *bilateral*, two-sided; *quadrilateral*, four-sided; *unilateral*, one-sided; and *lateral*, pertaining to a side.

Tripod combines *tri-* with Greek *podos*, "foot," found also in *podium*, the small raised platform on which the conductor of an orchestra stands; *chiropodist* or *podiatrist*, foot doctor; and *monopode*, a mythical single-footed creature.

IV

Are your classical (i.e., Latin and Greek) roots under control? Then, without checking with previous material, fill in two English words based on each of the roots below.

1. *monos*, "one"
   a. ....
   b. ....

2. *graphein*, "write"
   a. ....
   b. ....

3. *logos*, "word," "study," etc.
   a. ....
   b. ....

4. *mania*, "derangement"
   a. ....
   b. ....

5. *theos,* "god"
   a. ....
   b. ....

6. *bis,* "twice," "two"
   a. ....
   b. ....

7. *kyklos,* "wheel"
   a. ....
   b. ....

8. *gamos,* "marriage"
   a. ....
   b. ....

9. *oculus,* "eye"
   a. ....
   b. ....

10. *pedis,* "foot"
    a. ....
    b. ....

11. *sectus,* "cut"
    a. ....
    b. ....

12. *tri,* "three"
    a. ....
    b. ....

13. *lateris,* "side"
    a. ....
    b. ....

14. *podos,* "foot"
    a. ....
    b. ....

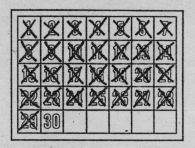

Words Change Their Meanings

You may remember the anecdote that was told of King George the First of England and Sir Christopher Wren, the architect of St. Paul's Cathedral in London. Upon the completion of the masterly edifice, the king told Wren that his work was "amusing, awful, and artificial." Sir Christopher was delighted with the royal compliment, inasmuch as three hundred years ago *amusing* meant *amazing, awful* meant *awe-inspiring,* and *artificial* meant *artistic.*

That is a dramatic indication of how the meanings of words change over the years. Latin and Greek, of course, are dead languages and are therefore static, but a language as vital and alive as English is in a constant state of flux.

In very olden days, roses used to "stink." This was not the fault of the flowers but of the word. In Old English "stink," and "stench" too, referred to any odor at all, good or bad. But since unpleasant odors make a stronger impression on us than others, and are, therefore, more often commented upon, the meaning of the word gradually shifted, and came finally to have only an unpleasant significance.

Similar shifts in meaning are occurring right under our eyes today. The words "smell" and "odor," when they are unqualified by adjectives, are beginning to gather about them disagreeable connotations. The phrases "what a smell" or "what an odor" certainly no longer refer to anything pleasant. Nowadays when our noses are pleased we have to resort to such terms as "scent" and "aroma." If these words become soiled someday, as they almost surely will, we may find ourselves resorting to "bouquet," a word now largely restricted to the distinctive aroma of wine.

"Villain" is another once respectable word that degenerated. Originally a "villain" was a farm laborer, or one who worked in a villa. Some philologists think the word was helped in its downward path by its supposed connection with the unrelated word "vile." Likewise, "hussy" is merely a contraction of the innocent word "housewife."

"Starve" used to mean "die." "Zest" was a piece of lemon peel. "Meat" in Anglo-Saxon was any food at all, as in the Biblical "If meat maketh my brother to offend. . . ." In the sixteenth century "specious" meant "beautiful," "stupid" meant "amazed," and "mortified" meant "deadened." And when the American settlers founded Plymouth, "naughty" still meant just what it sounds like—"good for naught"—and in the records of the colony we find the odd phrase "small and naughty canoes."

Change is of course one of the most reliable indications of a healthy and growing language. And no language has ever grown so luxuriantly or changed so radically as English, or its close cousin, our American language. It is changing day by day.

A few short years ago "broadcast" meant merely "to sow seed." Now it refers to radio and television. "Exotic" meant "foreign or strange," as "an exotic flower." Now we speak of a motion picture actress as being "exotic" when she is glamorous, and the use even of "glamour" in this sense is as new as motion pictures.

English, like time, marches on. What a word meant yesterday it no longer means today. The word "humor" formerly referred to one's disposition or state of mind, and still more formerly, to one of the four fluids of the body, and *still* more formerly, to moisture or vapor. Now it identifies that sense by aid of which we can appreciate something funny; and "funny," which once meant "laughable," now often means "queer or odd."

In the old days when we said a person was lying "prone," we meant, quite correctly, that he was lying on his face. Today, judging by newspaper photographs, he is usually lying on his back. In our present times a "fight" is often simply an argument; a "celebrity" is anyone who was in yesterday's gossip column. Today one can "climb up" as well as down; "lay" means "lie"; and "quite," formerly meaning "wholly," now, like "awfully," often means only "very." "Acclimate" has changed its pronunciation as well as its meaning, and is now usually used to show adjustment not only to weather or physical conditions, but even to one's friends. "Asylum," which comes from the Greek *asylon,* "no right of seizure," meant originally "a place of refuge." In modern times this word has been so corrupted that it has signified only "lunatic asylum."

So our language shifts, changes, grows, and is alive to the fingertips. There are new words for new times. If conditions today were identical with those of one hundred years ago, a "cabriolet" would still mean a "light, one-horse, two-seated carriage" as it did to our great-grandfathers, and not, as it did in the 1940s, a convertible coupé. (And today, of course, since language always becomes simpler, we call it, compactly, a "convertible.")

If civilization had not changed from Anglo-Saxon times, "curious" would still mean "careful," and "silly" would still mean "blessed."

Language changes, change is normal, and one hundred years from now many of the words whose meanings are suitable to the civilization of the twentieth century will probably undergo startling changes in order to adapt to the twenty-first.

You have come now to the end of your course. The next chapter will be a review test. You will have some idea of the progress you have made when we tell you that in these lessons you have added more words to your vocabulary than the average adult adds in ten to fifteen years. After the middle twenties, one's vocabulary growth virtually ceases unless a planned effort is made.

Remember how limited most of us are as to words. Nine native words, such as "it" and "the" make up one-quarter of our conversation. Add thirty-four more and you have half the words of our daily speech. That is, forty-three words do fifty per cent of our conversational work. There is so little you have to do to beat this average.

Write it large in your mind that a mastery of words is one of the essentials for success in every sphere of life.

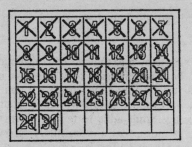

Your 30-Day Vocabulary Test

You have now added the greater part of five hundred usable and valuable words to your working vocabulary. It will be interesting to find out how many of them you are still sure of.

I

Check the word or phrase closest in meaning to each italicized word.

1. *gregarious* a. home-loving b. party-loving c. food-loving
2. *wanton* a. unrestrained b. desirous c. useful
3. *pander* a. fry b. cater to c. raise
4. *effete* a. worn out b. strong c. happy
5. *vicarious* a. actual b. second-hand c. vicious

II

Write five words ending in -*mania*.
1. ....
2. ....
3. ....
4. ....
5. ....

III

Write the verb, beginning with the initial letter indicated, that suits each definition.
1. To spend time in the country   R ....
2. To delay   P ....
3. To show disapproval   D ....
4. To exclude from social privileges   O ....
5. To be bright and witty   S ....

IV

Write the title of the doctor you would see for each of these troubles.
1. Eye diseases   O ....
2. Children's disease   P ....
3. Mental disorder   P ....
4. Skin trouble   D ....
5. Crooked teeth   O ....

V

What is the specialty of each of the following?
1. *Podiatrist* ....
2. *Gynecologist* ....
3. *Dermatologist* ....

4. *Oculist* ....
5. *Obstetrician* ....

VI

Check the word or phrase closest in meaning to each italicized word.

1. *panacea*   a. theory   b. information c. cure-all
2. *vindictive* a. revengeful   b. releasing   c. wise
3. *maudlin*   a. tearfully   b. angry   c. happy
                   sentimental
4. *misogynist* a. man-hater   b. marriage-   c. woman-
                                   hater   hater
5. *vitriolic*   a. glassy   b. caustic   c. mild

VII

What philosophy is implied by each of the following:
1. "There is no God."   A ....
2. "No one knows whether God exists."   A ....
3. "All virtue consists in self-interest." E ....
4. "Pleasure is the ultimate good."   E ....
5. "My country (religion, city, etc.) is
    superior to all others."   C ....

VIII

Name the field each scientist specializes in.
1. *anthropologist* ....
2. *geologist* ....
3. *archaeologist* ....
4. *embryologist* ....
5. *entomologist* ....
6. *ethnologist* ....
7. *etymologist* ....
8. *ornithologist* ....

9. *philologist* ....
10. *psychologist* ....

IX

Write the verb, beginning with the letter indicated, that fits each definition.

1. charge to   L ....
2. atone for   E ....
3. stagnate   V ....
4. cheat   M ....
5. beg   I ....

X

Check the correct definition.

1. *facilitate*	a. make better	b. make easier	c. make happier
2. *emulate*	a. imitate	b. deny	c. question
3. *gesticulate*	a. use gestures	b. use words	c. use sounds
4. *plagiarize*	a. steal literary property	b. torture	c. attack
5. *patronize*	a. cater to with condescension	b. defer to with respect	c. cater to with hesitation

XI

Write the meaning of the root and one English word built on it.

ROOT	MEANING	EXAMPLE
1. *monos*	....	....
2. *graphein*	....	....
3. *theos*	....	....

4. *bis*   ....
5. *tri*   ....

XII

Write the word that fits each definition.
1. Pathologic incendiarism   P ....
2. Fear of closed spaces   C ....
3. Sleepwalking   S ....
4. Hostility to father, with undue at-   O ....
   tachment to mother
5. Delusions of persecution   P ....

XIII

Check the proper word.

1. *Loss of memory*   a. insomnia   b. somnambulism   c. amnesia

2. *Incessant drunkenness* a. pyromania   b. kleptomania   c. dipsomania

3. *Trouble with imaginary ills*   a. claustrophobia   b. acrophobia   c. hypochondria

4. *Delight in inflicting pain on another*   a. sadism   b. cynicism   c. iconoclasm

5. *Pandering to the passions of people to gain political power*   a. anarchism   b. jingoism   c. demagoguery

XIV

Match the two columns by placing the appropriate letter of column B next to each word in column A. We have added an extra word in column B to make it more difficult.

	A.		*B.*
1.	disciplinarian	....	a. *coquette*
2.	boot-licker	....	b. *egotist*
3.	beginner	....	c. *martinet*
4.	conceited fellow	....	d. *sycophant*
5.	flirt	....	e. *atheist*
			f. *tyro*

XV

Proceed as before.

	A.		*B.*
1.	coin collector	....	a. *virtuoso*
2.	one with good taste in food	....	b. *philologist*
		....	c. *philatelist*
3.	beauty worshiper	....	d. *numismatist*
4.	student of language	....	e. *gourmet*
5.	skilled artist	....	f. *esthete*

XVI

Proceed as before.

	A.		*B.*
1.	man with one wife	....	a. *ornithologist*
2.	seer	....	b. *ethnologist*
3.	eye doctor	....	c. *clairvoyant*
4.	dabbler in art	....	d. *oculist*
5.	student of birds	....	e. *monogamist*
			f. *dilettante*

XVII

Write the word that fits each definition.

1. drowsiness or indifference   L ....
2. full to repletion   S ....
3. exhausted   E ....
4. boredom   E ....
5. haughtily contemptuous   S ....

XVIII

Write the meaning of the root and one English word built on it.

ROOT	MEANING	EXAMPLE
1. *anthropos*	....	....
2. *polys*	....	....
3. *philein*	....	....
4. *misein*	....	....
5. *pedis*	....	....

XIX

Match the two columns.

A.	B.
1. *taciturn*	a. learned
2. *esthetic*	b. tireless
3. *loquacious*	c. satisfyingly beautiful
4. *indefatigable*	d. talkative
5. *erudite*	e. silent

XX

Write the word whose meaning and initial letter are given.

1. Minor indiscretion   P ....
2. Boastfulness   B ....
3. Complicated and embarrassing situation   I ....
4. Warmongering   J ....
5. To shirk work by pretending illness M ....

XXI

Match the two columns.

A.	B.
1. introvert	a. truculent
2. inhibited	b. one whose mind is turned inward
3. diffident	c. quixotic
4. with impractical ideals	d. shy
5. overbearing	e. restrained

XXII

Check in each case the word *opposite* to the italicized word. Repeat: *opposite*, or *antonymous*.

1. *plebeian*   a. common   b. ordinary   c. distinguished
2. *inane*   a. wise   b. necessary c. useful
3. *wanton*   a. hopeful b. restrained c. lovely
4. *obsequious* a. brusque b. happy   c. sad
5. *crass*   a. rapid   b. refined   c. good

XXIII

Match the words of similar meaning in these two columns:

A.	B.
1. carelessly	a. *adroitly*
2. skillfully	b. *vociferously*

3. sourly
4. smoothly
5. loudly

c. *irascibly*
d. *glibly*
e. *cursorily*

XXIV

Choose from the following lettered list a word or phrase *opposite*—repeat, *opposite*—to each numbered word below the list. Write the appropriate letter next to each number.

a. useless
b. known to all
c. marriage within one's own race

d. solid
e. satisfactory
f. healthy
g. wasteful

h. necessary
i. stingy
j. wavering
k. respectful

1. *miscegenation*
2. *esoteric*
3. *nebulous*
4. *moribund*
5. *scurrilous*

XXV

Choose from the following lettered list a word or phrase *similar*—repeat, *similar*—in meaning to each numbered word below the list. Write the appropriate letter next to each number.

a. imaginary
b. hater of women
c. excessively fond of one's wife
d. stingy

e. overpatriotic
f. liberal
g. wasteful

h. homesickness

i. object of hatred
j. desirable
k. tireless

l. well-meaning

1. *parsimonious*
2. *catholic*
3. *uxorious*
4. *profligate*
5. *chauvinistic*

XXVI

Write "same" if the two words in a pair have similar meanings; "opposite" if they have opposing meanings.

1. *analogous*—similar ....
2. *ambiguous*—clear ....
3. *epigrammatic*—pointless ....
4. *euphemistic*—crude ....
5. *redundant*—repetitious ....

XXVII

Write the meaning of the italicized portion of each word.

1. dipso*mania* ....
2. *bi*ped ....
3. *tri*pod ....
4. *pod*ium ....
5. bi*cycle* ....

XXVIII

Proceed as before.

1. *anim*ate ....
2. *bene*fit ....
3. *fact*ory ....
4. *dict*ate ....
5. *un*ite ....

XXIX

Each one of the following five words is followed by a definition. Where the definition is correct, write "yes"; where it is incorrect write "no."

1. *ochlocracy*   ....   rule by a dictator
2. *omniscient*   ....   all-knowing
3. *fetish*   ....   object of hate
4. *facet*   ....   hope
5. *abstemious*   ....   gluttonish

XXX

Write "true" or "false" next to each statement.

1. *Chimerical* things are tangible.   ....
2. *Machiavellian* people are naïve.   ....
3. *Pariahs* are popular.   ....
4. *Diffident* people are generally *peremp-
   tory*.   ....
5. *Querulous* wives are happy.   ....

Allowing two points for each correct answer to the 155 items in the test you have just taken, it is possible to make a maximum score of 310. After checking with the answers below, read the results of your learning from the following table:

> 250–310 Excellent
> 200–250 Good
> 100–200 Fair
>   0–100 Poor

ANSWERS:

    I. (1) b;   (2) a;   (3) b;   (4) a;   (5) b

   II. dipsomania, megalomania, pyromania, kleptomania, bibliomania, egomania, nymphomania, Anglomania, Francomania, etc.

 III. (1) rusticate;   (2) procrastinate;   (3) deprecate;   (4) ostracize;   (5) scintillate

 IV. (1) oculist or ophthalmologist;   (2) pediatrician;   (3) psychiatrist;   (4) dermatologist;   (5) orthodontist

V. (1) feet; (2) women's diseases; (3) skin diseases; (4) eye diseases; (5) delivery of babies

VI. (1) c; (2) a; (3) a; (4) c; (5) b

VII. (1) atheism; (2) agnosticism; (3) egoism; (4) epicureanism; (5) chauvinism

VIII. (1) history of mankind; (2) rocks; (3) ancient relics or excavations; (4) unborn animals or children; (5) insects; (6) history of races; (7) derivation of words; (8) birds; (9) language; (10) human mind

IX. (1) impute; (2) expiate; (3) vegetate; (4) mulct; (5) importune

X. (1) b; (2) a; (3) a; (4) a; (5) a

XI. (1) one (monocle, monogram, monologue, monomania, monogamy, monotheism, monopode, monastery, monk, monopoly, monograph, etc.); (2) write (graphology, autograph, graphic, monograph, chirography, etc.); (3) god (theology, theocracy, monotheism, atheism, pantheism, theism, etc.); (4) twice, two (biped, bicycle, bicuspid, bilateral, binoculars, bigamy, bisect, etc.); (5) three (triangle, tricycle, tripod, trio, trinity, tricuspid, trisect, etc.)

XII. (1) pyromania; (2) claustrophobia; (3) somnambulism; (4) Oedipus complex; (5) paranoia

XIII. (1) c; (2) c; (3) c; (4) a; (5) c

XIV. (1) c; (2) d; (3) f; (4) b; (5) a

XV. (1) d; (2) e; (3) f; (4) b; (5) a

XVI. (1) e; (2) c; (3) d; (4) f; (5) a

XVII. (1) lethargy; (2) satiated; (3) enervated; (4) ennui; (5) supercilious

XVIII. (1) man, mankind (anthropology, anthropoid, misanthropy, philanthropy, etc.); (2) many (polygamy, polygon, polytechnic, polymer, polyester resin, polytheism, etc.); (3) love (philanthropy, Philadelphia, philately, philtre,

philosophy, bibliophile, Anglophile, Franco-
phile, Russophile, philodendron, philopro-
genitive, etc.);   (4) hate (misanthropy,
misogamy, misogyny, etc.);   (5) foot (pedestrian, pedal, pedometer, impede, expedite,
expedition, impediment, etc.)

XIX. (1) e;   (2) c;   (3) d;   (4) b;   (5) a
XX. (1) peccadillo;   (2) braggadocio;   (3) im-
broglio;   (4) jingoism;   (5) malinger
XXI. (1) b;   (2) e;   (3) d;   (4) c;   (5) a
XXII. (1) c;   (2) a;   (3) b;   (4) a;   (5) b
XXIII. (1) e;   (2) a;   (3) c;   (4) d;   (5) b
XXIV. (1) c;   (2) b;   (3) d;   (4) f;   (5) k
XXV. (1) d;   (2) f;   (3) c;   (4) g;   (5) e
XXVI. (1) same;   (2) opposite;   (3) opposite;
(4) opposite;   (5) same
XXVII. (1) derangement;   (2) twice, two;   (3)
three;   (4) foot;   (5) wheel
XXVIII. (1) mind or spirit;   (2) well;   (3) do,
make;   (4) say, tell;   (5) one
XXIX. (1) no;   (2) yes;   (3) no;   (4) no;   (5)
no
XXX. (1) false;   (2) false;   (3) false;   (4) false;
(5) false

One Last Word:
A Lifetime Habit

In one sense you have finished this book. In another we hope that you have just begun.

You have, perhaps, learned to know many words more intimately. And *any* new word that you learn in your life will add amazingly to your power to think. Once a man thinks—really thinks—he has little competition. You may remember that the Irish playwright George Bernard Shaw one time said that few people think more than two or three times a year. He claimed that he had made an international reputation by thinking as often as once a week! And please remember that there is no expedient to which a man will not resort to avoid the labor of thinking.

It will be more important now than ever before to shine up all the instruments in your kit that may prove to be the tools to success. We are coming out into a tough and tangled world. Those who are well-equipped will survive. Those who are not, may not. In almost every life, in every age, one gets what one asks for, and in this age of all others there will be very few alibis allowed.

There is not much of a secret to success. It is a great thing that is usually won by humble, routine methods. The mere decision you made to begin these lessons was an important step, for, as the Chinese say, "The journey of a thousand miles begins with a single step."

So continue with your word study. Watch for new words at all times. Never be content until you know the meaning of a strange one. Make it your own possession. Use it in a letter, in conversation. List it in your pocket notebook, with its common meaning, its pronunciation, and a sentence in which it is used. Have a little mental rehearsal on these words now and again while you are walking along the street. Carry on an imaginary conversation.

An intelligent argument, by the way, will give your new words a real workout. In such a challenge, a sharply accurate knowledge of the exact meanings of words is invaluable.

We can take particular and patriotic pride in mastering our speech. For ours is no longer the English language. It is the American language. Our language is as different from so-called English as South American Spanish is from the Castilian Spanish of Spain.

As a matter of fact, there is no true "English" language, as Scotland, Ireland, and Wales, and the various areas of England itself, all have their dialects. The Lincolnshire farmer and the Lancashire miner can't even understand each other. England, like almost every other nation in the world, is a mass of discordant dialects.

What we know as the "English" language is, much more truly, the "London" language, and the language of a particular part and class of London at that, as the inhabitants of Limehouse might laugh at the cockney dialect and the taxi driver would smile at the toff.

So there is every reason why you should take a deep and passionate pride in the American language. It has a beautiful unity throughout our land. No other country in the world one tenth our size can show such linguistic solidarity, nor any approach to it. This American language is your creation; it belongs to you, and the more you master it, the more secure you will feel in every aspect of your personal, social, and professional or business life.

Index

Index

Only the first appearance of each word in each chapter is indicated.